Ministering to Problem People in Your Church

What to Do With **Well-Intentioned Dragons**

Marshall Shelley

BETHANY HOUSE PUBLISHERS

a division of Baker Publishing Group
Minneapolis, Minnesota

© 1985, 2013 by Christianity Today, Inc.

Previously published as *Well-Intentioned Dragons*

Published by Bethany House Publishers
11400 Hampshire Avenue South
Bloomington, Minnesota 55438
www.bethanyhouse.com

Bethany House Publishers is a division of
Baker Publishing Group, Grand Rapids, Michigan

Printed in the United States of America

Library of Congress Cataloging-in-Publication Data is on file at the Library of Congress, Washington, DC.

ISBN 978-0-7642-1144-7 (pbk.)

Unless otherwise indicated, Scripture quotations are from the Holy Bible, New International Version®. NIV®. Copyright © 1973, 1978, 1984, 2011 by Biblica, Inc.™ Used by permission of Zondervan. All rights reserved worldwide. www.zondervan.com

Scripture quotations identified KJV are from the King James Version of the Bible.

Scripture quotations identified NIV 1984 are from the HOLY BIBLE, NEW INTERNATIONAL VERSION®. Copyright © 1973, 1978, 1984 Biblica. Used by permission of Zondervan. All rights reserved.

Though the case histories that appear in this book are used with permission, names and certain identifying details have been changed in some to preserve the privacy of the parties involved.

Cover design by Eric Walljasper

13 14 15 16 17 18 19   7 6 5 4 3 2 1

To those
scorched by dragons
but not reduced to ashes
nor hardened beyond feeling,
who in the face of beastliness
maintain their humanity
and divine calling,
this book is dedicated.

Contents

Foreword

I pastor a church in the Pacific Northwest; I am told from time to time that it is the most unchurched region in the whole of the nation. For some reason that holds appeal to people when it comes to faith and culture. As though a church in Portland is somehow immune to the realities of typical church culture because everyone is riding fixed-gear bikes and wearing scarves while drinking and eating local everything.

The truth is that any community of faith, whether in urban Portland or the Bible Belt, is made up of people—people for whom Christ died—some of whom you would rather punch than pastor on a given day. They may look different and talk different as you travel from city to city, but the same attitudes and actions have been present for thousands of years in communities of faith that we call the people of God.

I have a heart for pastors and their people. The reality is that all churches have challenging people. It is tempting to ignore difficulties and hope that they will simply go away. But in fact, to do so is to shrink back from caring for the flock, knowing that disruptive people and circumstances can wreak havoc on a community.

As a pastor myself, I recognize how myopic my view of the world can get. I don't spend lots of time reading blogs or staying up on the current fads and debates that loom large in our bubble of evangelicalism. I spend most of my time with my nose down in my own city and church trying to lead, preach, discern, and follow Jesus. One of the drawbacks of this life is that we don't often take time to look up and learn from other people or even listen to see how others are addressing the common challenges in which we find ourselves.

That is where Marshall Shelley's insights and observations come in. It is incredibly helpful to hear the stories, see the battle wounds, and collect the wisdom of other brothers and sisters who have traveled the road on which you find yourself. After many years with *Leadership Journal*, Marshall has a vantage point that we do not. He can look at the many stories, find the commonalities, and help give direction to leaders who often feel alone in the mess of ministry.

The good news is that you are not alone. You are not going through something that others have not had to endure. The people and challenges that you are in the middle of are not unique to you. And, perhaps most important, there is help and wisdom to lean into that most people are not talking about. The good news is that Marshall is addressing the mess found in the midst of the beauty that is the bride of Christ.

Rick McKinley
Portland, Oregon

Introduction

Church or Dragon's Lair?

Can you pull in Leviathan with a fishhook or tie down its tongue with a rope? . . . Its breath sets coals ablaze, and flames dart from its mouth.

Job 41:1, 21

Anyone who's involved in leading a church recognizes the irony: the community that gathers in the name of Jesus Christ is often populated by problem people who make things much, much harder for everyone. In this book, we call them "well-intentioned dragons."

Dragons, of course, are fictional beasts—monstrous reptiles with a lion's claws, a serpent's tail, a bat's wings, and scaly skin. They exist only in the imagination.

But there are dragons of a different sort, decidedly real. In most cases, though not always, they do not intend to be sinister; in fact, they're usually quite friendly. But their charm and earnestness belie their power to destroy.

Within the church, they are often sincere, well-meaning saints, but they leave ulcers, strained relationships, and hard feelings in their wake. They don't consider themselves difficult people. They don't sit up nights thinking of ways to be nasty. Often they are pillars of the community—talented, strong personalities, deservingly respected—but for some reason, they undermine the ministry of the church. In most cases, they are not naturally rebellious or pathological; they are loyal church members, convinced they're serving God, but they wind up doing more harm than good.

They can drive pastors crazy . . . or out of the church.

Some dragons are openly critical. They are the ones who accuse you of being (pick one) too spiritual, not spiritual enough, too dominant, too laid-back, too strict, too lenient, too structured, too disorganized, or ulterior in your motives.

These criticisms are painful because they are largely unanswerable. How can you defend yourself and maintain a spirit of peace? How can you possibly prove the purity of your motives? Dragons make it hard to disagree without being disagreeable.

Relationships are both the professional and personal priority for church leaders—getting along with people is an essential element of any ministry—and when relationships are vandalized by critical dragons, many pastors feel like failures. Politicians are satisfied with 51 percent of the constituency behind them; pastors, however, feel the pain when one vocal member becomes an opponent.

Sightings of these dragons are all too common. As one veteran pastor says, "Anyone who's been in ministry more than an hour and a half knows the wrath of a dragon." Or, as ministry veteran Harry Ironside described it, "Wherever there's light, there's bugs."

Research by *Leadership Journal*, a professional publication for church leaders, indicates that 80 percent of the pastors who read the publication need help with difficult people in the congregation.

And yet, many pastors enter the ministry totally unprepared for these attacks.

One pastor of a rural church considered an older deacon his closest friend in the congregation. The deacon, a farmer, generously shared produce from his garden and insisted on keeping the young pastor's aging Ford filled with gas from the tank behind the barn. The deacon also happened to be the church's biggest giver, providing more than 30 percent of the total budget.

One day the pastor, moonlighting as a school bus driver, had to discipline an unruly student. "I went strictly by the book," the pastor recalls. He dropped off the boy at home and told him to tell his parents the bus would not be stopping for him the next day. He reported the incident to the school superintendent and thought the matter was closed.

But the next day, the deacon, a friend of the boy's father, told the pastor he had overstepped his authority and completely mishandled the situation. "I think it's time you looked for another church," he said. "Your ministry here is over."

Even though the school board backed the pastor, within

six months the pastor was forced to resign because of the influence of that deacon, who chose to side with the boy's family rather than the pastor.

"I was shocked," the pastor says. "I felt betrayed and isolated. I was innocent, and yet this incident cost me my job. I wondered why I had been singled out for such abuse. I was totally unprepared for this.

"In seminary I learned how to discuss infra- and supralapsarianism, and yet in thirty years of ministry, I've never had to use that knowledge. But I've encountered lots of unreasonably angry people, people who made up their minds about things and didn't care to hear any facts to the contrary. I was never even warned such people would be out there."

By now he has learned that in ministry, criticism comes with the territory—some of it deserved, some of it unfair, all of it devastating for an individual who loves people and wants to minister to them.

This is a book about ministering while under attack. It was prepared after interviews with dozens of pastors who candidly described the difficult people they have faced. It is not a psychological study of problem people, nor is it an exhaustive catalog of the difficult individuals pastors will encounter. Instead it is a book based on the accounts of veterans of the dragon wars. The lessons offered are lessons of experience. They may or may not apply in other situations, but they at least provide a glimpse of the potential conflicts. Perhaps the wisdom of battle-tested veterans will prevent others from walking unaware into an ambush.

Though winged, fire-breathing dragons may be fictional, the stories you are about to read are not. Only the names, locations, and identifying details have been changed to protect present ministries. These are real-life stories of pastors who have succeeded, some who have failed, and all of whom have learned valuable lessons about continuing to minister amid the church's well-intentioned dragons.

1

Complex Conflicts

No matter what form the dragon may take, it is of this mysterious passage past him, or into his jaws, that stories of any depth will always be concerned to tell.

Flannery O'Connor

Despite Dwayne Wilson's sometimes brusque style and Virginia Wilson's high-octane zeal, Pastor Tyler Campbell considered the fifty-six-year-old church treasurer and his wife among the congregation's greatest assets.

Tyler discovered Dwayne's direct, no-nonsense approach right away. After his first service as pastor of Fair Glen Community Church, Tyler and his wife, Kristin, were standing at the rear door greeting worshipers. As Dwayne and Virginia Wilson came out, he took Tyler's hand firmly and said, "Our previous pastor was a good man, and he said you were a fine

fellow—the best we could possibly hope for in our situation."
Then he paused, looked Tyler in the eye, and concluded, "I
hope he's right."

Tyler tried not to dwell on the comment.

Fair Glen Community Church, just outside Cleveland, was
Tyler's second pastorate, and he and Kristin, both in their
mid-thirties, knew the value of the older, committed saints.
Only their faithfulness had enabled the church to survive the
lean years when attendance had dropped to fewer than eighty.

Both Dwayne and Virginia were deeply involved in the
church. Dwayne, a former elder, handled the church books
and taught an adult Sunday school class. Virginia led a morning home Bible study for women and enjoyed evangelism, or
"soul-winning" as she preferred to call it. She seemed to have
a knack for turning conversations toward spiritual topics,
even if she did come on a little strong for some members'
tastes.

The Wilsons were not conspicuously wealthy—as a general
contractor, Dwayne had been affected by the economy like
most in the construction industry—but they were generous.
Tyler learned that they had personally given the previous
pastor a new Cadillac as a retirement gift. And for the two
years the church was without a pastor, the Wilsons had single-
handedly covered the church's budget deficit at the end of
the year.

Dwayne was also a forceful Bible teacher. He spent lots of
preparation time listening to podcasts of his favorite Bible
speakers, following along in his cross-referenced study Bible.
His class was popular among those "in the second half of
life." He prided himself on taking the Bible literally, and

in class he would work through entire books of the Bible verse by verse, with only occasional detours to handle a topic such as prophecy in current events, the (subordinate) role of women, or spiritual gifts (at least those he considered still operative today).

Tyler cringed at some of Dwayne's dogmatic pronouncements. "I'm amazed how Dwayne insists on taking the Bible literally in some passages and how he explains it away in others," he once told Kristin. "His literalism is rather selective." But at the same time, Tyler was grateful for Dwayne's faithfulness and genuine desire to minister to his class.

Each year Dwayne would take some of the men from the class deer hunting in Michigan, and he had helped several families financially when job layoffs hit. The class was cohesive, said those who were in it; it was a clique, said those who weren't.

On the whole, Tyler was willing to put up with the 10 percent he questioned for the 90 percent that was positive in the class. Meanwhile, he began a class for younger adults, a group that had been somewhat neglected prior to his coming.

After Tyler's fourth Sunday, Virginia Wilson caught his arm following the evening service.

"Pastor, I met a young man who should be in your class," she said.

"Who is he?" Tyler asked.

"I met him in the shopping mall when I sat down to catch my breath," she explained. "Sitting next to me was this young man, and we struck up a conversation. One thing led to another, and he told me his story. He was arrested last year as a Peeping Tom, and he says he still struggles with those urges.

I told him he could be delivered if he'd turn his life over to Jesus. He seems interested, Pastor. He gave me his phone number, and I told him you'd give him a call. His name is Ernie."

She handed Tyler a card with the number.

"Uh, thanks," said Tyler. "Given the nature of the problem, I guess it would be better for a man to call."

"Oh, thanks so much, Pastor," Virginia gushed. "I just know the Lord is going to do mighty things through you." And she walked off before Tyler could say another word.

Tyler did call and offered to get together, but Ernie said no, he didn't think that was necessary. Tyler told Ernie about the church and their desire to be a place of healing and not judgment. And if Ernie ever wanted to talk about anything, Tyler's door was always open. Ernie said he might visit the church someday.

The next week, Virginia asked how the conversation went, and she was disappointed when Tyler told her.

"He seemed so open," she said, looking at Tyler with just a hint of accusation. "He needs Jesus."

"When a pastor takes the initiative like that, sometimes the person feels pressured," Tyler said.

"We can't expect *them* to take the initiative," said Virginia. "*We* have to reach out." True enough, Tyler agreed.

The following week before Sunday school, Virginia introduced Tyler to a young woman with wild, frizzy hair wearing blue jeans and a flannel shirt.

"This is Alicia," she said. "She wants to learn more about Jesus. She just got out of a treatment facility and is looking for a job. I told her Christ is what she needs. I'll leave you two alone so you can get acquainted."

Alicia spoke indistinctly, but Tyler found out she was on medication to control her emotional problems. Her story was hard to follow, but she said she had met Virginia at the shopping mall and she "got saved when I was little, but now I need Jesus to help me get better."

Tyler told her he was glad she had come, and he hoped she would become a part of the church because the body of Christ was a healing community. Alicia sat through class but left before church.

That night Virginia wanted to know if Tyler had helped her. "She's one who could really benefit from being in the church body," he said.

"I met her sister at the mall, too. You could really do her some good," Virginia said. "And by the way, you'll want to visit the Bonners' foster son this week. He's really depressed because his girlfriend dumped him, and he's not doing very well spiritually. And, oh yes, the Gibsons are having difficulties with their teenage son. I told them you'd call."

Each week, it seemed, Virginia told Tyler of another person she'd met who needed his ministry.

Tyler told Kristin, "Virginia can unearth more needy people at a shopping mall than anyone I know. Maybe it's because the only people willing to talk at malls are troubled people with no place in particular to go. She gets 1 percent into their problems, tells them Christ is the answer, and then turns them over to me."

When it happened again, Tyler told Virginia his primary job was to equip saints like her for this kind of ministry.

"That's true, Pastor," Virginia replied. "But I know you also have a burden for souls, and these people are ripe for the gospel. I'm locating needs so we can meet those needs and introduce the people to Christ." She was disturbed that Tyler wasn't more eager or effective in following up her leads.

Tyler and Kristin spent hours talking about the situation.

"I wish I could help those people she brings," said Tyler one night over supper. "But I get the feeling she wants me to preach at them and straighten them out in one conversation. Their problems are so complex—they are such high-maintenance people—that meeting their needs is a full-time job. I'd have no time for anyone else."

"Yes, Virginia thinks pointing out a problem is solving it," said Kristin. "She feels she's doing some great thing for God by spotting a need. She doesn't understand that meeting one need is more important than spotting fifty. Besides, the Spirit must lead both the giver and receiver of ministry. God has to be doing something in the person's life before our efforts will make a difference."

Tyler agreed. "She's an effective Andrew, but I can't possibly handle all the Simon Peters she's bringing. For one reason, not all of them come willingly—like the Bonners' foster son. He didn't want to see me; he needs a friend, not a pastor."

"Sounds like she promises them quick solutions to complex problems 'if you turn it over to Jesus,' which builds up some unrealistic expectations, too," said Kristin. "Poor Alicia certainly needs Jesus, but she also needs more treatment for her chemical disorders. I'm afraid Virginia doesn't understand that."

When Tyler tried to explain these things to Virginia, she misread his intention. "You mean pastors don't do evangelism anymore?" she said. Tyler tried to clarify, but when they parted, he knew she was unhappy. Her closing comment: "Well, they sure don't make pastors like they used to!"

It seemed like a minor disagreement at the time, but later Tyler saw his reluctance to handle Virginia's "projects" as the beginning of his growing alienation, not only from her, but also from all the Wilsons' disciples.

In the weeks that followed, Virginia did not bring any more problem people to Tyler's attention, but she brought Tyler to the attention of her Bible study. Several of the women told Tyler they were praying for "his vision for ministry." Another woman told Tyler she was quitting the group because the "hour of prayer" was "fifty minutes of talking about the pastor and ten minutes of prayer."

Tyler asked the elders about the criticisms. They downplayed the problem. Since each Tuesday evening he had been taking a different elder along on his visits to church newcomers, and often these conversations turned to the gospel at the core of Fair Glen, the elders said they felt Tyler was sufficiently evangelistic. And they were pleased at the results so far—several families had become Christians and were attending the church, and the elders were feeling more confident about sharing their faith.

Tyler hoped that with time Virginia's feelings would calm down, especially since the church was growing. After a year, Sunday morning attendance had grown from one hundred thirty to almost two hundred. And since the class Dwayne and Virginia taught was growing along with the rest of the church, Tyler hoped they would be happy.

They weren't.

Soon Dwayne joined his wife in criticizing "the direction of the church." Tyler heard reports that in Dwayne's class he was recommending preachers that "teach the Word with more meat than you usually hear in sermons around here."

Tyler decided to visit the Wilsons. Perhaps a pastoral call would mend fences. After talking about the growth in their Sunday school class, Tyler decided to be direct.

"Perhaps it's just me, but in recent weeks I've sensed a distance between us. I know my ministry style is not like the previous pastor's, but have I done something to offend you?"

"No, nothing specific," said Dwayne. "It's just that the church seems to have lost its first love. Virginia and I don't want to see our church become lukewarm."

Tyler fumbled for words. "I certainly don't want to be lukewarm, either. I'm committed to serving the Lord here, and I've been encouraged by the number of people who've joined our church and said they really sensed the Spirit of God at work."

He stopped. "I'm sorry," he said. "I don't mean to sound defensive. I do have a lot to learn about pastoring. Maybe you can help me. How do you think we can keep ourselves from becoming lukewarm?"

"We know you're evangelizing in your own way, Pastor," said Dwayne. "But we think you need to be more bold about it. Especially in the pulpit. You need to preach the Word. There are lots of kids in the church who are rebelling against their parents. You need to preach against that."

"And if I preached 'Honor your father and mother' from the pulpit, do you think the problem would be solved?" asked Tyler.

"If you preach it strong enough and often enough," said Virginia. "Scripture says, 'My Word shall not return void.'"

"You also need to preach against divorce," Dwayne said. "It's a real problem in our church."

Tyler knew all too well of the struggling marriages. He was meeting with four different couples, and in two cases, they had been able to reconcile their differences. In a third case, the husband left the wife for another woman and left the congregation. Tyler had encouraged the woman to stay in the church and continue her regular turn in the nursery. Some had questioned whether she should still be "in a leadership role," and Tyler defended her, saying she'd done all she could to reconcile. But a few couples from Dwayne's Sunday school class still weren't satisfied.

In a fourth case, physical abuse had been involved, and the couple, on Tyler's recommendation, had decided to separate temporarily while they continued to work on their problem. Tyler was encouraged by their progress, though they still had many obstacles to overcome. At least they were willing to keep working at it. Dwayne's class was upset by their separation, but Tyler, of course, couldn't share this confidential information.

"I hear what you're saying," said Tyler. "But I've learned there's a difference between *pronouncements* and the *process* God uses. In other words, condemning something from the pulpit doesn't eliminate it. Marriages are strengthened more by positive examples and support and dealing privately with problems than by preaching against divorce. Yes, parents ought to have authority in the home, and children should honor their parents, but I'm not sure putting your fist down is the way to convince kids of that."

Dwayne and Virginia looked dubious. When he left that night, Tyler hoped they at least trusted his motives, even if they didn't agree with his approach.

Unfortunately his peacekeeping expedition only fueled the fire. The next Sunday evening, Dwayne handed Tyler a four-page handwritten critique of his morning sermon.

"Here," he said. "You mentioned the other night maybe we could help you minister better. These are some suggestions on how you could have preached this morning's text."

"Thanks, I'll look them over," said Tyler.

Dwayne had carefully reconstructed Tyler's sermon outline and written comments under each point. The comments ranged from "Deuteronomy 17 is a good cross-reference here—let Scripture interpret Scripture!" to "That's not how this passage was handled by Dr. McMillan" (Dwayne's favorite West Coast Bible teacher) to "Too many uh's in here—a sign of too little preparation."

The next three Sundays in a row, he did the same thing. A recurring complaint seemed to be that Tyler wasn't as forceful as Dwayne would have liked.

One critique quoted Tyler's sermon: "We cannot prove the existence of God—even the Resurrection we accept on faith—but we can look at certain evidences and base our faith on those. Faith is deciding to believe even without scientific proof." Dwayne's comment: "Perhaps you cannot prove God's existence or the Resurrection, but Dr. McMillan can! Listen to podcasts #1635 and #1874."

Tyler tried to learn what he could from the criticism without letting it paralyze him, but he began to dread each Tuesday when he would sit down to begin sermon preparation.

His stomach would knot, and he knew that no matter what he said, Dr. McMillan had already said it better. Of course, McMillan was more a professor than a preacher, and Tyler didn't feel he could bring as much scholarship into the pulpit as McMillan did. Verse-by-verse commentary might be fine in a teaching situation, but for Sunday worship, Tyler wanted to accomplish something else: He wanted to create an atmosphere where love, acceptance, and forgiveness could flourish, where the church could become a source of warmth and outreach in the community.

He asked his elders about his preaching style, and they didn't see a problem.

"Don't worry about it," said Kristin that night as they were getting ready for bed. "Dwayne is comparing live performance to production. Those podcasts are from talks McMillan has given dozens of times. Of course they're polished. Plus, they have been edited. The weak illustrations have been taken out. If he stammers or says 'and-uh,' they take that out. And if he misses the mark sometimes, they don't even release that tape. Comparing you to McMillan isn't fair. It's like a man falling in love with the women in movies or in retouched photos—they never see those women without makeup or when they're sick. In a sense, people today prefer illusion to reality."

"Thanks," said Tyler. "Are you saying I'm sick?"

Kristin snapped him playfully with a towel.

Tyler probably could have endured the critiques if they had continued to come only from Dwayne. But before long, three of the men in Dwayne's class asked Tyler if they could begin selling Dr. McMillan's CDs and DVDs at a table in the foyer.

To keep the peace, Tyler approached the board with the suggestion. The board saw no harm in it, since Tyler's podcasts were already available, and approved making available resources "from any reputable Bible teacher, with board approval." In fact, the board spent more time discussing whether the church would owe UBI taxes (unrelated business income) on items sold than on whether this request was a subtle attack on Tyler. When they finally concluded that the resources could be sold at cost, thus removing any troublesome income, the board seemed to think its job was done. They hoped this would lead to peace within the congregation.

But even after that concession, Tyler began to sense in Dwayne's class a growing disapproval of his ministry. They had their own agenda for the rest of the congregation: a Statement of Christian Lifestyle. Tyler first heard about it when he made another peacekeeping visit to the Wilsons' home.

"The church needs to take a stronger stand against compromise with the world," Dwayne said earnestly. "We need to spell out clearly what is right and what is wrong."

"In what areas?" asked Tyler.

"Oh, you know. Divorce, gambling, smoking, drinking, tithing, things like that. We need to let people know what the Christian life is all about. That's discipleship."

"I agree we are to be distinct from the world," Tyler said, carefully choosing his words. "And one of the ways we are to be distinct, says John 13, is in our love for one another. I'm reluctant to spell out a specific list of do's and don'ts, because it's been my experience that those kinds of lists often result in a legalistic atmosphere. Love falls victim to law. People tend to look on the outward behavior without discerning the spirit within."

"But by their fruits you shall know them," said Virginia.

"Yes, we must stimulate one another to love and good deeds," said Tyler. "And I feel that happens best with an informal system of accountability, where we discuss these things with one another but leave the final judgments to God."

The rest of the visit was spent discussing whether the essence of faith rested more in attitude or behavior. Dwayne insisted that the church needed to be more directive. Tyler pointed out that the elders had discussed a lifestyle statement recently, and there hadn't been much enthusiasm. They'd felt that spelling out the minutiae of the law, especially as specifically as the Wilsons wanted, would cause more problems than it would solve.

Afterward Tyler felt they'd somehow missed the core of the problem, but he couldn't quite identify what it was. Whatever the cause, Dwayne and Virginia and the Sunday school class became increasingly restless with Tyler and the board.

During his sermons, no one sat grimly with arms folded; there were no cold, withdrawn glares. In fact, class members still nodded and smiled, but after certain statements, he noticed many of them glanced toward Dwayne and Virginia, as if to see whether or not they approved.

About this time, Tyler began suffering from colitis. The doctor told him there was too much acid in his system. All Tyler knew was that he was running to the bathroom seven times before the Sunday evening service, when he knew Dwayne would hand him another critique.

"Fortunately, I haven't had to leave the service . . . yet," he told Kristin with a smile.

His weekdays weren't affected until one day he overheard Dwayne telling one of the elders, "Our pastor really needs to concentrate on his personal spiritual growth if he's going to lead a congregation."

When the other elder said he thought Tyler seemed "pretty spiritually mature for his age," Dwayne continued, "Well, I'm hoping he's spending enough time in the Word. So many of his sermon illustrations have been coming from other books—last week he quoted C. S. Lewis, Dietrich Bonhoeffer, and Mother Teresa. I wish he'd let Scripture speak for itself."

After that, even yard work, which had been his release, was no escape from thoughts of the conflict at church. He couldn't even finish cutting the grass without having to make two or three trips to the bathroom.

Part of his frustration was that the elders knew Dwayne was grousing, but they didn't think it was serious. "He's always had dogmatic opinions," they said. "That's why we've allowed him to be church treasurer but not an elder." They didn't know, however, what those opinions were doing to Tyler.

The climax in the conflict occurred just a few months later, right after Tyler had served as guest speaker in a church on the other side of Cleveland.

When Tyler had candidated at Fair Glen, he had asked the elders if he, as pastor, could take two weeks a year to preach at other churches. He enjoyed that kind of ministry, and he felt exposure to other churches helped him minister at his own. The elders had agreed.

In November, Tyler took the two Sundays to minister at a church thirty miles away. He arranged to fill the pulpit the two Sundays he would be gone, and he had one of the elders lead the midweek prayer service. He still managed four pastoral calls and a funeral for Fair Glen during that week.

But on the 15th, when he usually got his paycheck, there was nothing in the mail. Two days later, when it still hadn't arrived, he called Dwayne, the church treasurer.

"Say, Dwayne," Tyler said jokingly, "you don't happen to have my check, do you? My kids are getting hungry."

Dwayne didn't laugh. "No, I don't. You were off the last two weeks, weren't you?"

"Well, I spoke elsewhere on the Sundays, but I cleared it with the board. And I was here all week."

"I didn't hear anything about you being paid," Dwayne said. "I figured if you're off somewhere else, you get your money from them."

"Maybe this is something for the board to decide," Tyler said, suddenly feeling the effects of colitis. "Let's sit down together tonight after prayer meeting."

That night, after Dwayne told why he'd withheld the check, one board member said, "We gave the pastor permission to preach at these meetings. I don't see any problem." The others nodded in agreement.

"Well, what should I do?" Dwayne demanded.

"Write him a check," said the board chairman, Ray McGregor.

"For how much?"

"All of it," said Ray.

"Okay," said Dwayne. "But some people come to this church to hear the pastor, and if he's not here, they might not come back."

Tyler apologized to Dwayne for the misunderstanding and said he was flattered Dwayne considered his preaching an attraction. Dwayne didn't smile.

Two Sundays later, the stress caught up with Tyler. As he walked to the pulpit that morning, he saw Dwayne and Virginia in the fourth row, and he dried up. He couldn't preach. He paused before the congregation for an uncomfortable moment and then said, "I've been going through some tense, distressing times in recent days. And to be honest with you, I've got nothing to say. I'd like to ask Ray McGregor, our church chairman, to come up and pray for me and for all of us this morning."

As Ray prayed, some phrases from Psalm 102 came to Tyler's mind. "My heart is blighted and withered like grass. . . . I eat ashes as my food and mingle my drink with tears." When Ray sat down, Tyler quoted the verse and explained how it sometimes describes the human condition with stunning clarity.

"Now is such a time in my life," he confessed. "And when that happens, I know I must trust God in the same way as did the psalmist, who, though no relief from his suffering was in sight, nevertheless drew strength from the One who could see the end from the beginning. In times like this, all we can do is look to God, even when he seems silent, and say with the psalmist, 'In the beginning you laid the foundations of the earth, and the heavens are the work of your hands. They will perish, but you remain; they will all wear out like a garment. . . . But you remain the same, and your years will never end.'"

As he spoke, he looked at Kristin, and she returned his gaze steadily, confidently.

This unsermon lasted only five minutes, and the service closed early. Tyler was feeling better, but he tried to leave quickly out the side door. He wasn't quick enough. Virginia Wilson grabbed his arm just as he got outside.

"My twelve-year-old grandson was sitting beside me today," she said. "And he heard the pastor say he doesn't have victory in his life. I ask you, how can my grandson have victory when it's not demonstrated even in our worship services? I don't want you to speak that way again."

"My dear Virginia," Tyler said, "Jesus loves you, and I do, too." It was trite, but he couldn't think of anything else to say, and it left her confused just long enough for him to escape.

Tyler got into his car wondering if it wasn't time to resign, move back to Vermont, and look for work doing something, *anything,* else. Here at Fair Glen, he couldn't preach; prayer was a struggle; and even pastoral care, his favorite task, seemed impossible to do with integrity. *Maybe Virginia is right,* he thought. *I have no answers to this problem, and if I have no answers for myself, how can I offer help to someone else?*

The next time church elections were held, Tyler did persuade the nominating committee not to put Dwayne up for treasurer again. He had served for fifteen years, but the flap over the paycheck convinced the board he should probably take a sabbatical.

Dwayne, predictably, was hurt. He accused Tyler of trying to drive him out of the church. Tyler assured him that was not his intent. He set up a weekly breakfast with Dwayne to try to build a better relationship, but there was no warmth, no healing. The wounds were still too fresh. And in church business meetings, Dwayne made sure a dissenting voice was heard loud and clear.

When several church women wanted to begin a preschool and day-care center to minister to the neighborhood, Dwayne made an impassioned speech that day care encouraged women to leave their children and seek employment, "which undermines the very thing we're commanded to teach—that women belong at home with their children. Anything else is a violation of God's intended structure for the family. Plus, as the former treasurer here, I know we can't afford it." He had enough influence to sway the vote, and the proposal was defeated.

A few months later, the elders were discussing whether or not one of the younger men, Paul Dewey, should be nominated for a board position. The constitution didn't specify age limits, but elders had always been more than forty years old (most more than sixty). Paul was only twenty-nine, but he had demonstrated "maturity and a servant's heart," as Ray McGregor put it. Paul, an electrician, had acquired and installed the church's sound system without charge. He was continually volunteering whenever work needed to be done around the building. At Fair Glen, three elders were assigned responsibility for maintaining the facilities and purchasing necessary equipment. Ray suggested Paul would be an excellent choice for one of those positions.

At one of their breakfasts, Tyler decided to bounce the idea off Dwayne.

"I think we ought to have the whole congregation praying about this, Pastor."

"Well, the idea is just in the thinking stage. We're trying to weigh the pluses and minuses," said Tyler.

"Pastor, elders have an important leadership function. Scripture calls them elders for a reason—they are supposed to be older. I heard Dr. McMillan say recently that the Greek word for elder is *presbuteros*, and that means older men. I think we should stick to what the Bible says."

"Interesting point, Dwayne. We'll have to study that."

"If you're contemplating something this major, it should be prayed about by the entire body."

"I agree, Dwayne. And it will be—at the appropriate time. But you and I both know that there are times when discretion means you don't go public before you've done your home-work. If the elders decide *not* to recommend this course of action, getting people upset about the issue would only hurt the ministry."

Dwayne was unconvinced, but Tyler hoped at least he was pacified.

He wasn't. The board still had not made a decision when, at the next business meeting, just before entertaining the motion to adjourn, chairman Ray McGregor asked if there was any other business. Dwayne stood up and said, "Mr. Chairman, do I understand that the elders of this congregation are considering installing young people as elders?"

The rustling of papers and coats as people were getting ready to leave suddenly stopped. Dwayne waited for a response.

The room was silent. Tyler stifled an urge to shout, *You're the one who talked with me about this issue, Dwayne. Why are you asking now?* But he remained quiet and let Ray handle the question.

"I don't know about the term *young people*, Dwayne. We have discussed how old elders should be, but no decision has been made as yet. Okay, do I hear a motion to adjourn?"

"Just a minute," Dwayne interrupted. "Why is it even being considered when the Bible clearly indicates that all elders are older? Aren't we a Bible-believing church?"

"Dwayne," Ray said firmly. "This isn't the time to get into a detailed discussion. The question can't be answered quickly. The elders have been appointed the spiritual oversight of this body, and the elders are seeking God's direction in many areas, and if and when a specific proposal should be made to the congregation, you'll be the first to know. Good night, everyone."

Tyler was so angry he slipped out a side door and went home without speaking to anyone. As he and Kristin lay in bed that night and reviewed the events of the past three years, he said, "I'd sure love to have a *normal* church. Why can't we just get along like human beings?"

The next day, Tyler and Ray met to talk. They decided the problem needed to be tackled head-on, that since Dwayne had made an issue of it already, they might as well go public with a tentative proposal that elders must be at least twenty-five years old.

Over the next three months, the issues were debated in a series of congregational forums, several elders reported on the biblical evidence, and rejoinders were accepted from the floor, giving Dwayne ample opportunity to state his case, which he did with fervor. These meetings were expressly billed as *not* decision-making sessions but times for seeking the Lord's guidance.

After three months, another business meeting was called, a vote was taken, and the congregation unanimously approved an amendment to the constitution that elders must be at least twenty-seven years old. It was something of a compromise, though neither side enjoyed the process of negotiation.

If this story were a fairy tale, someone would wave a magic wand and disagreements would disappear, leaving the principals at peace and the church prospering. In real life, however, dragon stories go on; the ends don't tie quite so neatly.

Two weeks after finally agreeing on the age issue, Dwayne approached one of the board members and said, "I wonder if our pastor is praying enough. Being a spiritual leader is an awesome responsibility for such a young fellow, and he really needs to maintain a quality devotional life."

When the elder mentioned the conversation to Tyler, Tyler felt like he'd been kicked in the stomach. "I wish he'd spend as much time praying for me as he does worrying about me," he said.

Even church discipline has got to be easier than this, he thought. But there was nothing to discipline Dwayne for. He wasn't rebelling against God; he said he was desperately trying to obey Scripture, at least as he understood it.

The problem was that he and Tyler were on different wavelengths. Dwayne was primarily literal and dogmatic in his understanding of Scripture, latching on to one or two specific verses as the clear answer to any question; Tyler was primarily contextual, looking at the literary, historical, and theological context of Scripture and trying to apply the "whole counsel" of God to today. Dwayne thought the church should emphasize more Bible knowledge; Tyler thought the people already knew more Bible than they could obey, that sermons should emphasize living out their knowledge.

Under such circumstances, Tyler is discovering that reconciliation takes a long time. Thanks to the support of the elder board, his job is not threatened, even if his health is. Tyler and Dwayne have shared countless breakfasts and apologized to each other, but in many ways, their situation is like two people trying to reconcile after a divorce. Neither wants to be hostile, but neither can forget the past. Rebuilding trust is much harder than building it. After conflict and separation, after two people have so seriously injured each other, even after apologies have been made, restoring spontaneity and carefree affection doesn't happen overnight.

Tyler is continuing to minister with the weight of a not-quite-resolved situation. He has preached sermons on forgiveness, as much to himself as to the congregation, but the feelings don't go away.

He has told Dwayne, "This may be your greatest spiritual test—to learn love and forgiveness when it's hard to do." And that seems to be getting through. Both he and Dwayne are willing to continue trying to work together. Tyler consciously tries to think well of the Wilsons and understand their viewpoint, and Dwayne sends Tyler occasional notes of encouragement for particular sermons or specific instances of pastoral care to one of the Wilsons' friends.

The easy way out for Tyler would be to encourage Dwayne to leave, or to look for another church himself. But he is not willing to admit defeat—he believes warmer relationships are possible, even when the climate is still chilly. Nor does he see separation as the answer to confronting dragons.

The rest of this book deals with various kinds of dragons, their tactics, and the ways to handle them. But from the beginning a premise stands clear: The goal in handling dragons is not to destroy them, not merely to disassociate from them, but to make them disciples. Even when that seems an unlikely prospect.

2

Identifying a Dragon

Qualifications of a pastor: the mind of a scholar, the heart of a child, and the hide of a rhinoceros.

Stuart Briscoe

Dwayne and Virginia Wilson represent only one kind of well-intentioned dragon, a complex and durable species. Many other kinds have been sighted within the church—some merely nuisances, others serious threats to church life.

Before looking specifically at some of the most common tactics of dragons, it might be helpful to catalog some of the varieties inhabiting the church. All of the following have been reported by working pastors.

Dragon Species

The Bird Dog. Four-legged bird dogs point to where the hunter should shoot. The two-legged Bird Dog loves to be the pastor's eyes, ears, and nose, sniffing out items for attention. "If I were you, I'd give Mrs. Greenlee a call. She has some marital problems you need to confront." Or, "We need more activities for the youth." Or, "Why doesn't the church do something about . . ."

Most pastors respond to Bird Dogs by saying, "The Lord hasn't said anything to me about this, but it sounds like a good idea. Obviously you're concerned, and that's usually a sign the Lord is telling you to do something about it." Those genuinely concerned will take up the challenge. Bird Dogs, however, will grumble, "That's your job, Pastor. I'm just calling your attention to something important."

Of particular bother is the Superspiritual Bird Dog. This purebred strain is more likely to point out things that leave the pastor feeling defensive and not quite spiritual enough. "The Lord has laid on my heart that we need more of a prayer ministry in this church." Who could argue otherwise? Or, "We need to develop more discipleship and maturity within this congregation, wouldn't you say, Pastor?" Or the ever-demeaning, "Our church just isn't being fed enough by the Word," with its unspoken implication that the pastor and the preaching are coming up short.

These people like to give the impression they have more spiritual perception than anyone else. "It's more irritating than threatening, but it always shakes my confidence," says a pastor in Virginia. "I find myself questioning whether I really have the mind of Christ, whether I'm fulfilling my pastoral responsibilities as I should. Especially when I'm tired and feeling overwhelmed already, this kind of person really gets me down. I don't need more Bird Dogs. I need more shooters!"

The Wet Blanket. If you've heard the phrase "It's no use trying" or its close cousin "It's too much effort," you've probably spotted the Wet Blanket. These people have a negative disposition that's contagious. They spread gloom, erase excitement, and bog down the ministry. Their motto: "Nothing ventured, nothing lost."

A pastor in upstate New York describes one such obstructionist couple, who live next door to the church. Since it's a joint parish and the pastor lives twelve miles away, this couple informally oversees building maintenance. "Last winter, I called them each Wednesday afternoon asking them to turn on the heat in the church building for prayer meeting that night," the pastor recalls. Inevitably, the couple would refuse. "We don't need heat," they would argue. "It's too expensive, not enough people will show up, and those who do can sit for an hour in their coats."

In business meetings, they exhibit the same attitude toward any step of faith. "We tried that before, and it didn't work" is a familiar refrain. Because of their pessimistic certainty, people are reluctant to vote against them.

The Entrepreneur. Just the opposite of the Wet Blanket, the Entrepreneur is enthusiastic. He's the first to greet visitors at the church and invite them to his home. Unfortunately, in addition to being enthusiastic about the church, he's equally eager to sell them vitamins, bee pollen, cleaning products, or whatever product he's currently offering.

"We were losing people because they felt victimized," says a minister in Wisconsin. "It got so bad I had to mention in a sermon that we can't make each other the objects of our enterprise. We also had to put a notice in our church directory that this list is not to be used for business activity."

The Drill Instructor. This is the person who comes from the union steward school of diplomacy and speaks with an exclamation point instead of a period.

He (or she) is right, and everyone else is wrong, and he doesn't mind saying in the middle of a church business meeting, "I don't like what you said!"

"All of the church's salaries are out of line; pastors are paid too much these days!" said one such dragon in a business meeting with the pastor's entire family present.

This kind of person is a steamroller who flattens anyone in his way with his overwhelming insistence that his is the only right way to see things. Negotiation is a dirty word; compromise, unspeakable.

If this person is on a church board that has settled a sensitive issue privately, but he wasn't completely satisfied with the decision, he's likely to bring it up again in a congregational meeting. While most people believe "It's better to light a candle than to curse the darkness," this type of dragon lights the candle near the propane because he'd rather see some fireworks.

The Anonymous Blogger. These dragons may claim to be "trying to save our church," but they do it by posting comments and accusations and interpretations on the Internet without attaching their names. Their main accomplishment is heightening a climate of suspicion and dissatisfaction.

Without identifying themselves, they air the church's dirty laundry. Often there's no way to evaluate the truthfulness of the rumors they spread.

"A website was reporting what various church staff members and other leaders supposedly said in private conversation," said one pastor. "But when it reported on what I supposedly said, my words were twisted, taken out of context, and made to imply something I never intended. It made me skeptical of the way everyone else's comments were reported."

Because of the widespread use of electronic tools for escalating conflict, we will spend an entire chapter on dealing with this type of dragon.

The Fickle Financier. This person uses money to register approval or disapproval of church decisions. Sometimes he protests silently by merely withholding offerings, though more often he lets others know that he's not giving.

"I can always tell when I've made an unpopular decision," says one Maryland pastor. "Missions giving goes up, the general fund scrapes bottom, and it's usually right before the quarterly business meeting. They think they're punishing the pastor."

Others, however, because of the amount of their giving, realize their money means clout, and they directly manipulate people and programs.

In one small church in Oregon, the owner of the local school bus company and his family represented 50 percent of the church's income. When the new pastor went in for his first haircut, the barber said, "Oh, you're at the church Mr. Peabody owns." The pastor couldn't tell if he was joking. He later discovered he wasn't.

Mr. Peabody expected the pastor to keep regular office hours and managed to find some excuse to call almost every morning at 9 and again shortly after 11:30 to find out if he was there.

"That was just one symptom of the control he exerted," says the pastor, who has since left, though the calls continue with his successor. "It was a hardship, but there's no solution unless you're willing to stand up to him and risk losing half your funds, a loss I didn't feel the church could survive."

A Georgia pastor faced a similar situation.

"In my first church of thirty members, the largest contributor threatened to stop contributing if such and such wasn't done. I said, 'I'm sorry you feel that way, but you don't judge this church—God judges all of us.' The church wasn't for sale. It cut the ground out from under him."

These are just a few of the dragons ministers encounter. There are many others too numerous to mention in detail:

- *The Busybody*, who enjoys telling others how to do their jobs.

- *The Sniper*, who avoids face-to-face conflict but picks off pastors with potshots in private conversation, such as the cryptic "Be sure and pray for our pastor. He has some problems, you know."

- *The Bookkeeper*, who keeps written record of everything the pastor does that "isn't in the spirit of Christ."

- *The Merchant of Muck*, who breeds dissatisfaction by attracting others who know he's more than willing to listen to, and elaborate on, things that are wrong in the church.

- *The Legalist*, whose list of absolutes stretches from the kind of car a pastor can drive to the dress code for the worship team to the type of disposable coffee cups the church uses.

Any of these can inhabit a given congregation.

How do you know a dragon if you see such behavior? You can't tell by looking. Dragons can be as friendly and charming as non-dragons. Sometimes you can't even tell by listening . . . at first. People can criticize, voice dogmatic opinions, tangle with others, and yet not be dragons.

The distinguishing characteristic of a dragon is not *what* is said but *how* it's said. Even though dragons are well-intentioned, sincerely doing what's best in their own eyes, the characteristic that marks a dragon is that they are never quite with you. Often they have a spirit that enjoys being an adversary rather than an ally. They have a consistent pattern of focusing on a narrow special interest rather than the big picture, which leads to following tangents rather than pursuing a balanced church life. They persistently shift the church off course.

Theirs is a spirit quick to vilify and slow to apologize. Dragons usually cannot bring themselves to accept responsibility for something that has gone wrong, and hence, they resist asking anyone's forgiveness.

This spirit, of course, is difficult to discern quickly. It can only be judged by observing the person's effect on the larger ministry of the church. As 1 Timothy 5:24 says, "The sins of some are obvious . . . ; the sins of others trail behind them."

Perhaps the greatest threat from dragons is not their direct opposition. It's more intangible. They destroy enthusiasm, the morale so necessary for church health and growth. People no longer feel good about inviting friends to worship services. The air is tense, the church depressed, and everyone is aware of "us" and "them."

The effect on pastors is equally serious. They sap pastors' energy and, just as damaging, goad them into *re*acting instead of acting.

"The real problem isn't so much their overt actions," observes a veteran pastor. "But they divert your attention and keep you off guard even if they never openly oppose you. You find yourself not planning, not dreaming of the future, not seeking a vision for the church—you're just trying to survive from day to day."

If pastors become preoccupied with the dragons, afraid to challenge them, or at least too concerned about "fighting only battles that need to be fought," they often lose their spontaneity and creativity. Change is stifled, growth stunted, and the direction of ministry is set by the course of least resistance, which as everyone knows, is the course that makes rivers crooked.

If the first casualties in dragon warfare are vision and initiative, the next victim is outreach. When a pastor is forced to worry more about putting out brush fires than igniting the church's flame, the dragons have won, and the ministry to a needy world has lost.

Habitations of Dragons

Where are the places dragons are most likely to appear? After interviewing dozens of pastors who have survived numerous encounters, a few observations seemed to recur. These warnings are not intended to arouse suspicion or distrust of potential friends. They're offered simply to help clarify some of the dynamics of dragon behavior.

The worst dragons may be, in the beginning, the pastor's strongest supporters. Often the opposition seems to develop from among those responsible for calling the pastor.

One pastor, now in his fifth church, says, "A wise old minister told me the person most likely to become your severest critic is the person who picks you up at the airport on your candidating visit. So far he's been right three out of five."

They're not always members of the pastoral search committee, but dragons often seem to emerge from among the people influential in calling the pastor.

Why? Perhaps their expectations are greater. Perhaps they are more emotionally tied to the church and feel more ownership. Perhaps they feel their leadership threatened by a new pastor. Perhaps they're simply the stronger personalities. Whatever the reason, they often become the loyal opposition, or in some cases, not so loyal.

Another pastor, a church planter, observes a similar tendency even in situations without a search committee. "The people who were part of the core, the first four families, were among those who eventually became disenchanted with me. They saw me as *their* pastor, and as the congregation grew, one of them told me, 'These new people don't love this church like we do.' And when I inevitably spent less time with the charter members to concentrate on others, they grew distant and eventually sharply critical of me."

Dragons often work overhard initially at befriending you. If you list the people who make an appointment to see you in the first month of a new pastorate and another list of those unhappy with your ministry a year later, you'll be amazed at the overlap. Often when they first come, they want to "share a personal concern" or let you know "the *real* situation in the church." What they really want, of course, is to co-opt your allegiance for their agenda or special interest.

Other times, certain individuals will give overgenerous gifts. "One man in my congregation took me aside and slipped me a $100 bill every month. Another offered to buy me a new suit each year," said a pastor in Des Moines. "I didn't refuse at first, but then I realized these gifts had strings attached. These men had a political end in mind. They were trying to own me. I've since turned down these gifts and asked them to make the contribution to the church's benevolence fund, instead."

People who try overhard to be friends are sometimes genuine, but other times they just want to be in the inner ring, to gain the pastor's ear, to increase their influence in the church.

Dragons often compare you to their former pastor. Dragons have invariably had previous church experience, either at another church or in the present church with the previous pastor. Dragons are virtually nonexistent among those for whom you are the first pastor.

One small-town pastor in the Midwest, who counts among his congregation the widow of the former pastor, was confronted by her one Sunday morning.

"I tried to call you this week," she said. "Your wife told me it was your day off. I'll have you know my husband never took a day off in twenty-three years of ministry." The pastor stifled an urge to point out her husband had also died at age forty-five.

The prior experience of a congregation affects churches of every size and denomination. Unless the congregation has been without a minister for a *long* time, the spirit of the former pastor is very much present. Whether the former pastor was loved deeply or intensely disliked, the congregation's priorities certainly have been shaped by the predecessor. Some will want a clone; others will want a sharp contrast.

Interestingly, just because people praise their former pastor does not mean they're going to become dragons. In fact, they are probably not as dangerous as those who've developed a habit of criticizing past ministers. They may be revealing their lack of respect for the pastoral position.

"When I first came to Birch Ridge Presbyterian," says the current pastor, "I got so tired of hearing how wonderful my predecessor, Rev. Becker, had been. They called him 'Old Brother Beck,' and they adored him. But that turned out to be a good thing. When I had been there four or five years, their loyalties shifted my way. It just took a while to be accepted as their leader."

If they brag about the former pastor, it may be cause for thanks, not irritation. It's safer than the members skinning him alive. Members' attitudes about their former pastor can, in time, transfer to you.

Dragons thrive when the church's formal authority and informal power structure don't align. Whenever the church office holders, elected or appointed, are different from the unofficial but widely recognized power brokers in the congregation, dragons seem to multiply.

One Minneapolis pastor who teaches a seminary course in practical theology asked his students to draw a chart of the lines of authority in their home churches. The students all drew neat boxes for various committees and boards with lines running cleanly from one to another. Then he asked them to diagram the *real* decision-making process. One student turned in a sheet with lots of small circles around the edge connected to one large egg-shaped circle filling the center of the page. The large circle was labeled "Ralph."

No church government is perfect. Dominant personalities may not be spiritually qualified for leadership. And no church structure can ever perfectly fit the changing human relationships within a congregation. But the extent of the mismatch between formal and informal leadership will determine the amount of tension in the congregation. One inevitably must adjust to the other.

Dragons are often bred in counseling. Those you've counseled, or their family members, frequently become either eternally grateful for your help or infernally resentful that you know too much.

People often seem to become distant with those who become too familiar with their intimate struggles. In counseling, if the problems are not resolved, counselees are often uncomfortable facing the counselor later—not only does he know their problem, he knows it hasn't been dealt with. When this happens with a pastor, often the people withdraw from the church—either physically or emotionally—or else they begin working to oust the pastor.

Even if the pastor maintains a good relationship with the counselee, sometimes family members resent his involvement.

"The wife of one of my deacons came to see me about their marriage difficulties. Her husband refused to admit there was a problem, but his relationship with me became tense because he knew what his wife had been telling me. Eventually he became one of the individuals instrumental in demanding my resignation," says the pastor, who was forced to leave. "I can't help but think at least part of the breakdown in our relationship was due to his discomfort knowing that I had been listening to his wife about their marriage problems."

Dragons often sensed a call to the ministry at one time. Surprisingly, most pastors indicate they do not have as many problems with those currently in Christian work as they do with those who should be in ministry and aren't.

"I have several parachurch workers, preachers' kids, and retired ministers in my congregation, and they're my most supportive members," says an Illinois pastor. "I've learned to lean on them when I need to. They understand ministry and appreciate what the church is doing.

"The problems come from those who've sensed a call and haven't followed it. It's the frustrated, armchair pastors who want to run the church."

Another pastor reports his dragon is a former missionary who took a job in the home office and is suddenly away from a direct people ministry.

The only solution? Finding a place where these people can minister directly to needy people.

"We had a young couple who'd committed themselves to going overseas during a missions conference, but they never went," says the Illinois pastor. "They were a source of dissension until we identified what they were feeling and put them in charge of tutoring some inner-city kids. Now they feel great about the church."

The old adage "If they have a problem, give 'em a job" isn't bad if the job is meaningful and especially if it's in an area where God has called them before. If you can tap the cause of the frustration, help them recognize it, and love them in spite of their abrasiveness, they can be transformed from dragons into highly motivated allies.

These are by no means all the situations conducive to dragons. Nor do these conditions mean dragons will necessarily appear. Many pastors are able to minister effectively in all of these situations without arousing the wrath of problem people. It does help, however, to understand the factors at work.

Understanding Dragons

How do dragons get that way? Rarely is it a conscious choice to become beastly. Hardly ever are dragons so bad that they see themselves as dragons. Other than the pathological sadists, not many people in human history were mean because they enjoyed it.

"I have never met a man who wanted to be bad," writes George MacLeod. "The mystery of man is that he is bad when he wants to be good."

In the church, most dragons see themselves as godly people, adequately gracious and kind, who hold another viewpoint they honestly believe is right.

Unfortunately, sincerity without self-examination is no excuse. Remember the old joke about the proud mother who thought every member of the marching band was out of step except her Freddy? Even with intense self-examination, not all the factors are clear. In dealing with dragons, it's helpful to understand some of the underlying causes of their behavior.

First, people do battle because they *feel* so strongly. Emotions are often more powerful than logic. In an ideal world, people who differ would sit down together in faith and good fellowship, and after some friendly debate reach an agreement based on Scripture, sound theology, and calm reasoning. But we know that doesn't happen. If a person is argued into submission or politically subdued in one area but the underlying emotional need isn't met, he'll simply create another headache somewhere else.

When a person complains, "I'm not being fed" or "You're not meeting my needs," sometimes it's out of frustration or out of a sense of neglect or isolation. Theological answers to relational tensions rarely address the real issue.

"I used to have very little patience with these people," says a Nazarene pastor, "until I noticed I do the same thing. Another pastor, a good friend of mine, accepted a denominational position, and I began to resent him because when he was in town he always seemed to have time for other pastors but not me. I found myself criticizing him, finding theological reasons to disagree with him. But I wasn't *judging* him, I was *mad* at him."

In a similar way, the criticism of a dragon may spring more from anger than differences over the immediate subject. And sometimes the anger is not specifically directed at the pastor but at the situation.

"The guy who's overlooked in his company and has been passed over for promotion five times can make the dirt fly in the church," says a pastor in Alabama. "I've struggled most with people who resist all types of authority, not just pastoral leaders. They've never met an executive or a supervisor they liked, and they see the pastor as a supervisor. They don't have much control in their jobs, but they're determined to exert some power in the church.

"It's taken ten years to get close to these people, and interestingly, it's happened as a result of them seeing my failures in a situation where I wasn't the one controlling the outcomes."

Second, despite their sincerity, people cannot overcome their human nature. All of us sometimes act out of sheer spite, even while justifying our actions to ourselves.

In John Miller's book *The Contentious Community*, he compares the church to a children's choir gathered in the sanctuary to sing praises to God. "Innocence and guile are perched on the edge of the platform, waiting to burst forth in song or shove some unsuspecting freckle-faced being to an ignominious landing three feet below. And it isn't that Bonnie is innocent and Bobby is full of guile; it is that innocence and guile, the ideal and the real, are coursing through the veins of each."

Or, as Saint Augustine pointed out with barbed wit, "The innocence of children may be more a matter of weakness of limb than purity of heart."

The church, indeed every Christian, is an odd combination of self-sacrificing saint and self-serving sinner. And the church, unlike some social organizations, doesn't have the luxury of choosing its members; the church is an assembly of all who profess themselves believers. Within that gathering is found a full range of saint/sinner combinations. Ministry is a commitment to care for all members of the body, even those whose breath is tainted with dragon smoke.

3

Personal Attacks

Resolved: that all men should live for the glory of God. Resolved second: that whether others do or not, I will.

Jonathan Edwards

Seldom are your critics actually disappointed with you. They are usually disappointed with themselves, their circumstances, or God. You are simply a convenient target.

Wayne Cordeiro

Dragons are best known for what comes out of their mouths. At times their mouths are flamethrowers; other times the heat is not apparent, but the noxious gas does the damage. Sometimes the words are calm but crafty. Dragons' tongues may be smooth, but they are usually forked.

The tongues of church dragons also wreak destruction. James compares the tongue to a small spark that sets a great forest ablaze. Pastors also know the dangers of verbal sparks in a tinder-dry congregation. In most cases, the fire eventually singes the pastor in some sort of personal attack.

These personal attacks, however, rarely start with a direct clash. The would-be attacker usually begins with covert warfare, going to others in the congregation seeking those of like mind, those who deal in dissent.

Then, like the serpent in Genesis 3, the strategy is one of planting insidious questions in people's minds, at first seemingly innocent questions, but with the result of raising doubts about the pastor's competence, credibility, ministry, or motives. One pastor's experience illustrates the complexities of dragon warfare and the damage these personal attacks can bring.

The Vulnerable Ministry

Gordon Landis first became aware of the undercurrents of dissension during the building program. He knew any building program puts stress on a congregation and produces criticism, but in this case, one of his decisions, made with good intentions, was coming back to haunt him.

In the six years since Gordon and his wife, Sarah, had planted Pebble Mountain Baptist, the church had grown to 250 members, and everyone recognized the need for a facility. That wasn't the problem. Neither was fund-raising— members were generous, and the church had to take only a $250,000 mortgage, excellent for a small town in Tennessee.

His tactical blunder was trying to save money by building with mostly donated labor. Decisions had to be made as they went along, and too many people were involved in minor issues, which led to second-guessing.

Once the disagreements began, they seemed to snowball, and inevitably the criticisms began to be directed at Gordon. One deacon's wife in particular, a charter member of the church, began questioning carpet colors, floor plan, and square-footage requirements. After Gordon ignored or overruled her three or four times, her criticisms turned toward his ministry.

"Pastor, your preaching has changed over the last six years," said Maureen.

"I hope so," Gordon replied. "If you don't do some changing in six years, you're dead."

"That's not what I mean," she persisted. "You're not as effective. You're not reaching people like you used to."

Gordon privately asked his deacons for their perceptions. None of them agreed with Maureen. Sarah thought the comments were unfair. But Gordon couldn't quite shake the nagging doubts. His confidence in the pulpit wavered ever so slightly.

Soon Maureen began taking a different approach.

"Pastor, this church is growing, and it's getting too big for you to be able to stay in touch with everyone. I want to help you. I'll watch the church for you, especially for needs in people's lives. You need to know what's happening."

"I don't want any witch hunts," said Gordon.

"Oh, no. Of course not," said Maureen. "I wouldn't do that. I'm just going to help you stay close to the people. I insist."

To pacify her, Gordon agreed. *I don't have to jump every time she points the finger,* he thought.

Maureen turned out to be an excellent detective. She certainly seemed to know what was going on. Most of her reports were accurate. She alerted Gordon to a personal dispute between two deacons, and he began picking up the clues in business meetings. Eventually he was able to help them reconcile. When she reported that a contractor in the church was fudging on building code requirements, Gordon had lunch with him and asked in general terms how his faith affected the way he did business. The conversation eventually led to the man admitting to his shoddy practices and promising changes.

The instance that caused Gordon to regret his unleashing of Maureen was, ironically, one he knew about before she did.

Paul and Pat Parsons were having severe marital problems. Pat had moved out and was dating another man, often staying overnight at his apartment. Gordon had met with Paul and Pat both individually and as a couple, and he was encouraged—Paul admitted his anger issues and violent outbursts. Pat was no longer demanding an immediate divorce, and she seemed at least open to the idea of reconciling. But she wasn't ready to move back in with Paul.

That's where it stood when Maureen rushed in to tell Gordon that church discipline had to be exercised because of Pat's adultery. Gordon told Maureen he was dealing with the situation through counseling and that he was making progress. Maureen agreed to let him handle it privately—reluctantly, it seemed to Gordon.

Three weeks later, Pat finally agreed with Gordon that she would stop dating her boyfriend, though she wouldn't admit her affair was wrong. Paul was beginning to show signs he might be able to forgive her adultery and work at being a better husband.

But things weren't moving fast enough for Maureen. She called each deacon, told what she knew about the affair, and demanded that unless Pat confessed her sin, repented, and asked forgiveness, she should be asked to leave the church. After three deacons called within an hour to ask what was going on, Gordon called Maureen to ask why she'd not let him handle the situation.

"If you're not going to deal with this sin, Pastor, then I have to take it openly to the deacon board. You've shirked your responsibility to tell her to repent or leave the church."

Gordon tried to say that the situation was moving in the right direction, and that going public would only undo the fragile ties he'd been able to knit together. "Please don't upset the apple cart," he said. "The notoriety can only hurt the couple and the church."

"I'm sorry. I can't do that," Maureen said. "It's open sin; it has to be dealt with openly. If she hasn't confessed by now, she won't. Leopards don't change their spots."

Half-truths, like half-bricks, Gordon knew, are more dangerous because they fly farther.

"Maureen, please don't tell me what the Holy Spirit can't do."

But Maureen wouldn't listen. She swayed the board members to take action. Not wanting to violate issues of confidentiality, Gordon didn't feel free to go into detail about the dynamics of his counseling sessions with Paul and Pat. But he did indicate that things were improving. The deacons, however, felt they had to act on what they did know. In a split vote, the deacons decided to discipline Pat. Since the sin had become public knowledge, and since Pat still wasn't admitting her affair was wrong, justifying it in her own mind, they felt they had to act publicly.

Sadly, after the church action, Pat gave up on her marriage and moved in with her boyfriend. Paul stopped coming to church at all.

Maureen emerged from the episode stronger than ever, a prophetess of sorts. She began telling her women's Sunday school class that she didn't see how God could bless the church with growth until it got stronger leaders. When the church continued to grow numerically, taking in thirty new members the next twelve weeks, she began questioning whether the church could grow "in maturity."

In the following months, she made issues out of the women's organization, the lighting in the sanctuary, the church kitchen schedule, and the furnishings in the nursery. Gordon began gaining a whole new appreciation for the imprecatory psalms.

When she stood up in prayer meeting and pointed out that the pastor's views of the Second Coming differed from those of her favorite Christian TV talk show host, Gordon blew up.

"I admit it. I lost my cool," he says. "I told her I got my theology from the Bible, not from a blow-dried talking head. I said the trumpet of the Lord will rouse more people than the troupes of well-rehearsed singers with their Christian Muzak that puts me to sleep.

"I admitted I wasn't as attractive as the TV personalities, and I'm sure I'm wrong on a lot of things, including some fine points of doctrine, but I've been called to this church, and I'm ministering as faithfully as I can. Even if I can't compare with other preachers, at least I'm here, I'm yours, and I'm available twenty-four hours a day."

The thirty faithful at prayer meeting were motionless, stunned at the outburst.

Maureen, somewhat flustered, said, "I'm sorry, Pastor. I didn't mean to belittle your ministry. Maybe we should apologize to each other and start over."

Gordon didn't feel he had anything to apologize for, but he took a deep breath, accepted her apology, and said, "Yes, I'm ready to be friends and go ahead with the Lord's work."

After that, Maureen didn't openly criticize Gordon, but what she began telling her friends was "I don't get anything out of the sermons, but he's the pastor, and he'll be here until God moves him on."

After one service, she told Gordon, "Pastor, you're a good people person, but your preaching doesn't meet my spiritual needs. It doesn't have the depth I need. Don't worry, though. I'm not going to leave, even though I could be fed elsewhere. I need to stay here and help you." Gordon tried to suggest gently that ministry is a two-way street, that she could minister most effectively in a church she felt good about, and that she needn't stay at Pebble Mountain if she was unhappy. But Maureen wasn't about to leave.

She did, however, continue to make life difficult.

Each Sunday during the pastoral prayer, Gordon was in the habit of praying with eyes open, looking at the congregation he was uplifting in prayer. Every time his glance rested on the third pew from the rear, right side, he saw Maureen sternly staring back, her arms folded and her eyebrows knit. Soon he consciously avoided looking at the right side of the sanctuary. And some days he didn't really feel like praying at all.

During sermons, Maureen's posture changed. She opened her Bible and studiously lowered her head for twenty minutes of fervent Scripture reading. If she wasn't going to get anything out of the sermon, she might as well read the Bible—at least that was the message communicated to Gordon.

Gordon's married daughter, Marcia, and her husband, Hank, sang in a semiprofessional bluegrass band, "The Rainbows," with another couple from the church, Don and Peggy. The four of them spent a lot of time together ("too much," according to Maureen).

When The Rainbows won a statewide contest and were scheduled to sing in Nashville at a Sunday evening gospel and bluegrass festival, one of the deacons suggested the Sunday evening service be canceled so the pastor could see his daughter perform, and besides, the deacon happened to be a bluegrass fan, too. The deacons all agreed it was terrific for the pastor to support his daughter this way, and service was canceled.

Maureen, despite her husband's vote to the contrary, didn't care for the decision. "God comes first," she told Gordon. "He takes precedence over you, your family, or anything else. God doesn't want you to cancel a church service, especially for a country-western concert. Those concerts are pretty loose morally, Pastor. Your ministry is slipping."

By this time, Maureen had been joined by two other women, one of them another deacon's wife. They were concerned that their pastor went to movies; they didn't approve of his taste in music; in short, they didn't care for Gordon's moral judgments.

Gordon didn't feel he had anything to defend, and the deacons didn't seem to take the women's criticisms seriously, so Gordon tried to ignore the comments, but they nagged and dragged, sapping his excitement for ministry.

One of the dangers of chronic critics, however, is that you don't know when to ignore them and when they should be taken seriously. Like the boy who cried wolf, they numb you with so many complaints you don't know which ones to act on. When Maureen and her two assistants came to Gordon to tell him they thought his daughter was living an immoral life, at first he thought they meant her singing. But they had something else in mind.

"I think Marcia is spending too much time with Don," Maureen said. "She can get him to do things for her that his wife can't get him to do. It doesn't look good. I think they're having an affair."

Gordon's fatherly instincts wanted to rush to his daughter's defense; his pastoral instincts wanted to say, "The apostle Paul says you who are spiritual should try to restore those who sin—have you talked directly with Marcia about this?" But Gordon knew arguing with Maureen wouldn't solve anything, and he thought a confrontation between Maureen and Marcia would only be ugly, so he agreed to Maureen's demand—"Okay, I'll talk with her about it."

Marcia denied any involvement with Don and, thought Gordon, was appropriately incensed at the very suggestion of an affair. Marcia was ready to confront Maureen and demand she retract these "lies." Gordon tried to calm her, telling her to ignore Maureen, that she often spoke without knowing the full truth. When Maureen called Gordon again, he defended his daughter.

Two weeks later, however, on Friday afternoon, Marcia went to the home of one of the older deacons, a man she trusted, and confessed she had been intimate with Don and that she'd lied to her father about it.

"You've got to tell your dad immediately," he said. "He has his livelihood, his service for the Lord, his reputation all on the line for you."

Marcia did confess to her father, and "it nearly killed me," Gordon says. "I immediately got on the phone to the three women who'd come to me, and I told them, 'You were absolutely right, and I didn't believe you. I'm sorry.'"

Two of the women graciously accepted Gordon's apology and said they believed he hadn't known about it. Maureen, however, accused Gordon of knowing all along. Gordon hung up a broken man.

He didn't go to church that Sunday. He had given his resignation to the board chairman, and he and his wife stayed home, held each other, and cried.

At that service, however, unknown to Gordon, Marcia stood before the congregation, admitted her sin without naming Don, and asked for forgiveness. The church tearfully and unanimously accepted her back.

The chairman then read Gordon's letter of resignation and said, "We're not going to vote to accept or reject this resignation right now. We'll do that at a special business meeting next Sunday night, but let's spend the rest of the service in prayer for Marcia, for our pastor, and for our church."

The following week was a blur for Gordon. Don met with the deacons, he confessed his sin, and they considered the matter closed. The families of the women involved in the investigation, however, including two deacons, threatened to pull out "and take half the congregation with us" if the pastor's resignation wasn't accepted. The other deacons felt the pastor need not resign for the sin of a grown, married daughter.

Hopelessly deadlocked, the board set up an ad hoc committee to hear testimony in the case. The three families expressed their dissatisfaction with Gordon's ministry; others defended his record. The procedures lasted three weeks. Gordon and Sarah were left in limbo. He'd told the board he would not return to the pulpit until the church decided one way or another on his resignation.

"I didn't know if I could return even if they invited me back," Gordon remembers. "My spiritual life was devastated. When you're standing knee-deep in mud, it's hard enough to reach up for the Father's hand, and I was face-down in the mud."

Gordon searched the want ads for jobs: truck driving, retail sales, real estate, anything. He even drove by the navy recruiter's office wondering if he could still qualify as a chaplain.

After twenty-one days of deliberation, the ad hoc committee reached a decision. The entire committee, except the three, came to Gordon and Sarah's house and asked them to remain. They assured Gordon of their 100-percent support. They told him the three couples had agreed to leave. Gordon gratefully accepted their invitation to be in the pulpit the next Sunday.

"I'm a fairly emotional person," says Gordon. "I cried all the way through the meeting, and most of the others on the committee were crying, too."

For two more years, Gordon Landis remained at Pebble Mountain Baptist, despite the stories circulated through the other churches in town by the three families who left. Newcomers would visit the church and tell Gordon, "We heard about the troubles here, but we thought we'd see for ourselves what the church is like."

The small-town atmosphere did not let the scars heal quickly. Marcia and Hank's marriage could not survive the strain; they divorced, and Marcia moved to Nashville. Don and Peggy stayed together but moved to Birmingham. For Gordon, the delayed stress was as bad as the original stress had been.

"Several times Sarah and I would be in a restaurant, and across the room would be one of the three families," says Gordon. "They'd be talking with someone else, and in our paranoia, we were sure we were the subject of conversation. I began to become somebody I did not want to be. Always a people person, I started to withdraw from personal relationships. I liked to trust people, but I began to back off.

"We no longer talked freely about our children, afraid of the inevitable painful questions. We could no longer bare our souls to our friends. I stopped asking the probing pastoral questions because I didn't want to know about any more problems."

This isn't pastoral care, thought Gordon. *I'm violating one of my vows before God.*

One Saturday morning, Gordon went to the church and walked up and down the aisles of the sanctuary, arguing with God.

I don't want to be mad at you, but I don't like where you've got me, he prayed. *You say you're in control of all things and that all things work together for good for those who love you, but things aren't working together too well for me. I've got a church, but my ministry is lifeless.*

"Suddenly God graphically made me realize that if there was distance in my relationships, it was because *I* had moved," says Gordon. "I knew I had to get back." He went home, and he and Sarah knelt by the couch, praying for freedom to care for others and committing the results to God. "He gave us that peace, that release to be ourselves."

Despite resolving the matter in his own mind and soul, four years after the crisis, Gordon realized his ministry would probably be more effective elsewhere, and he is now pastoring another church. The attack of the dragon, while not fatal, had inflicted a wound that would take years to heal.

The Mind of the Minister

This is only one account of the effects of infighting with dragons. As with many struggles in life, the battle lines are not always clearly drawn. You don't know when to attack, when to withdraw, or when to call for help. All you know is your head pounds, your blood pressure rises, and the tension doesn't go away.

How does a leader deal with personal attacks, accusations against family, character, ministry, motives?

Specific strategies will be discussed in later chapters, but before discussing steps of action, the essential attitude must be spelled out: *When attacked by a dragon, do not become one.*

No encounter with a dragon is a complete failure unless one fights venom with venom. No victory is worth winning if it forces us to become bilious. To paraphrase John Claypool, if I become a beast in order to overcome a beast, all that reigns is beastliness. Paul's familiar words in Romans 12 apply even to the mean and ugly attacks from church members: "Do not repay anyone evil for evil. Be careful to do what is right in the eyes of everyone" (v. 17).

This doesn't guarantee victory; it does guarantee success. The dragon may have his way; the job of a Christ-one is to live Christ's way.

Joseph offers a challenging model for responding to personal attacks. He was sold into slavery by his own brothers, and his father didn't even know he was alive. Then, just as he began to rebuild his life, he was betrayed again by Potiphar's wife, who lied about him, destroyed his reputation, cost him his job, and had him imprisoned.

Somehow through the dark years, however, Joseph maintained his trust in God. And when he met his brothers years later, he could say, "You meant it for evil, but God meant it for good" (see Genesis 50:20).

This freeing attitude is possible only through the Spirit. That doesn't mean, of course, that we continue in conflict that grace may abound. God forbid!

It is almost impossible to love those we fear. We do neither ourselves nor the dragons a favor by allowing them to wreak destruction unchecked. We don't meekly bow before the most dominant personality. If the dragon remains some-one to be feared, love has lost. We have to take what steps we can to prevent the future fearful consequences, but then, having done everything "as far as it depends on you [to] live at peace with everyone" (Romans 12:18), our fears must be exchanged for faith, which makes possible love for enemies, love even for dragons.

We are to be, Jesus said, wise as serpents and innocent as doves (see Matthew 10:16). Streetwise peacemakers. Compassionate confronters. Above all, patient disciples who understand that God can redeem even the worst situation for his glory.

4

Electronic Warfare

It is a sign of a perverse and treacherous disposition to wound
the good name of another, when he has no opportunity of
defending himself.

John Calvin

My thoughts trouble me and I am distraught
because of what my enemy is saying, . . .
for they bring down suffering on me
and assail me in their anger.

Psalm 55:2–3

Email, texting, Twitter, blogs, Facebook, and other electronic forums have complicated and magnified the potential for dragons to exert their influence. Sometimes church

leaders get drawn into the wars of online words, and before they know it, they've inadvertently done more harm than good.

One of the most dramatic cases of electronic warfare began with a negative Google review of a church in the Pacific Northwest. A former member of that church posted:

"Although this church touts itself 'Garringberg Grace Community,' I found very little 'grace' there. This is a legalistic church where if you don't do things their way (the 'only' way), you will have challenges. Garringberg Grace is known to shun former members/attendees without giving an explanation. You will be fine in this church if you never question the elders or pastor. If you do not believe, worship, and evangelize 'their way,' they will let you know you are not a true Christian. Be wary of churches that proclaim they are one of the few remaining churches that preach the Word. Do not be deceived."

More negative reviews followed. Other church members noted the negative Google reviews and tried to rebut them with positive reviews. One example: "All believers are called to do the work of evangelism (Matthew 28:19–20). Many churches today exert too much effort entertaining goats instead of feeding sheep. Churches should be preaching repentance and faith (Acts 20:21). Many of these churches have zeal for God, but not according to knowledge (Romans 10:2). Garringberg Grace holds fast the faithful Word, that we may be able, by sound doctrine, both to exhort and convict those who contradict (Titus 1:9). Our pastor diligently preaches the gospel and faithfully upholds the Word of God. My wife and I have been blessed by over ten years of his preaching and guidance. Our salvation is nearer than when we first believed (Romans 13:11)."

As often happens in open online forums, the vocabulary got nastier and more mean-spirited. Anonymous posts began appearing such as this one: "Garbage church. No interest in teaching the Word of God. Instead the pastor just wants to mindrape the members for personal gratification."

Eventually the pastor and the church elders waded in: "To Whom It May Concern: Almost a year ago the woman who wrote the review and her husband were biblically put out of Garringberg Grace Community with a group of families and individuals who were engaged in ongoing divisive slander. After attending many churches and leaving them in a similar manner, the group has now splintered. Many of those in this fractious group no longer attend church at all. It is sad to see that she remains steadfast in her destructive behavior. For obvious reasons we exhort you to heed the following Scriptures: Proverbs 6:16–19, 28; Romans 16:17–18; Titus 3:9–11. It is our prayer that there will be no more wood thrown upon the fire of contentiousness, strife, and discord. It is our prayer that the fire will go out and that the body of Christ at Garringberg will be able to press on 'in the one Spirit, striving together as one for the faith of the gospel' (Philippians 1:27). It is our prayer that those who started the fire and have cut, stacked, and stoked much wood upon it will repent for God's glory and their blessing. If you have any questions, please contact the pastor and elders."

When the negative reviews continued, eventually the pastor and church leaders appealed to Google to remove what they considered the most offensive comments. And, indeed,

Google did remove some of the reviews, including the one that started the sharp criticisms. But removing reviews on one website didn't solve the problem.

The author of the original review launched her own blog, "Garringberg Survivors," where she posted more of her own criticisms and stories of "spiritual abuse" from others who had been hurt by the church. The blog became a gathering place for those with complaints about the way things had been done at this church and others where people had felt mistreated.

In one post, the blogger wrote: "I was abused as a child. I remember reaching out to adults who 'dissed' my story. They either didn't believe me or did not want to get involved. I get very angry when people sit by idly and allow abuse to continue. I remember so many times in my childhood asking God, 'Why is this happening to me?' Could God be using my childhood story for a higher purpose? I don't know. All I know is that somehow this story has taken off. I did not plan this. When I posted the review, it was to give my story, share my church experience so that people could come to their own conclusions. I did it because I wanted to protect others from what we had gone through.

"Years ago, I went through counseling and one of the most difficult concepts for me to fathom was that adults heard my story and did nothing. Let me repeat, they heard the story and *made the choice* to do nothing. There were things they could have done with that information. But they didn't want to get involved. That is what ate at me after the year we left the church. Nobody was doing anything. There was no one to turn to. The elders noticed no problems—we had already asked them. There was no one above the pastor to call. He was at the top of the chain. Google was the only thing I could do. I felt if the information in my review could help just one family, just one person, then it was worth it."

After three years of attacks, including charges that the church practiced spiritual abuse and that a known sex offender in the church was given access to children and the nursery, the church leaders went to court, suing the blogger and two other codefendants for defamation.

This, of course, only heightened the sarcasm and venom on the Internet: "Well, this is mighty Christlike of the leadership of this church to sue a woman over a damned Google review," wrote one anonymous commenter. "Talk about immature temper tantrums! This is insane. Stop now before the Internet destroys your church. Wait, oops, too late."

The church, however, proceeded with the lawsuit.

"It's an attempt to ruin us," the pastor said. "They have said the worst possible things you can say about a pastor, about a church."

While free speech is protected under the First Amendment, defamation is not. The church had to prove the blogger's words were both false and written to harm the pastor's reputation. The blogger's attorneys argued that she had a right to free speech and that there was no evidence of malice in the posts online. They argued that she wrote the truth to the best of her knowledge.

The judge decided in the blogger's favor, and the church had to pay for the blogger's court fees.

The old saying goes, "Sticks and stones can break my bones, but words can never hurt me." But in this case, words wound up costing the church damage to its reputation and $50,000 in legal fees.

It's not entirely new that church fights spill over into the public arena. After all, Martin Luther nailed his ninety-five theses to the door of the church in Wittenberg, Germany, thinking he was inviting semiprivate academic debate over some points of practical theology. But his intentions notwithstanding, nailing those theses to the church door was the equivalent of posting them on the Internet today. The ideas were out there for everyone to read.

Church leaders cannot control what their people write on the Internet. In extreme cases, as the Garringberg story illustrates, a church can dismiss people from the congregation, but that won't stop them from writing whatever they want on their blogs.

As a result, churches are on notice that they need to be wise in their responses to electronic attacks. Responses that are too defensive may backfire and only escalate the hostilities and extend the damage.

Potential for Misunderstanding, or Understanding

Michael Brown was the director of the Federal Emergency Management Agency (FEMA) in 2005 when the overwhelming force of Hurricane Katrina swamped both New Orleans and, apparently, the abilities of FEMA to provide disaster relief.

In late August, on the day Katrina struck, Brown sent an email to a friend that read, in part, "Are you proud of me? Can I quit now? Can I go home?" He later wrote to a friend on September 2 that he could not meet her because "I'm trapped now [as FEMA head], please rescue me." And at another time, "If you'll look at my lovely FEMA attire, you'll really vomit. I am a fashion god."[1]

By November, Brown's email messages were made public after an investigation into the federal government's handling of the Katrina disaster. Critics claimed that Michael Brown's emails displayed a lack of professionalism. While there were other factors that played a part in this political drama, Brown eventually resigned from his position, a casualty of his agency's shortcomings and the power of email to reach far beyond the intended recipient.

The same dangers lurk in the church, as one North Carolina pastor discovered.

"The email seemed a simple request," he said. "In a sermon I'd mentioned seeing the *Matrix* movies. That had piqued the curiosity of this young woman, who'd read a review of the movies on a Christian family-values website and now wanted to know if I thought it was appropriate for Christians to see R-rated movies."

The pastor shot off a quick reply—saying that he saw nothing wrong with watching an R-rated movie if you can handle it, and many mature Christians find such "real-life" exposure helps rather than harms their spiritual walk by getting them out of "the Christian bubble."

"I hit the send button without another thought," he said. "By the end of the day, however, things had flared into a B-grade horror flick.

"Her reply charged me with condoning pornography, violence, and perversity. I was the one 'in the bubble,' she said, and I needed to consider what the Holy Spirit inside me was thinking while I watched such filth."

Her email ended: "Obviously I'm at the wrong church. You cannot be my pastor. I have no respect for you. You'll never see me at church again."

"The whole thing left me stunned," said the pastor. "My first reaction was *Ouch*. Did I mention she was thirteen years old? *(Double ouch.)* And often babysat my daughter? *(Triple ouch.)* Then her mother and brothers dove in. The whole family e-agreed: I was an arrogant jerk with a questionable commitment to Christ who needed to repent of viewing such seedy segments of the culture. What I'd thought to be solid relationships deteriorated instantly."

What had gone wrong? Several things, starting with wrong assumptions (which are easy to make with email).

"I'd big-headedly assumed the teen believed I was right and she wanted to watch R-rated movies herself," the pastor said. "I was wrong. She hadn't sought confirmation—she wanted me to explain myself. I'd failed to read the seriousness in her question. My flippant reply assumed that what was a small matter for me would be a small matter for anyone else.

"I re-read my initial email response to her through the eyes of someone sincerely in love with Jesus whose commitment to holiness led her to question our R-rated culture. When I did that, I couldn't believe what I had written. Of course it had offended. It would have been a miracle had it *not* offended.

"The smartest thing I'd done, it turns out, was to copy the teen's mother on my reply. I'd initially not planned to pull the mother into the conversation—after all, it was just a simple question. I cringe to think what it would have looked like had I not cc'd the mother and suggested the teen discuss such matters with her mom, 'the person most responsible for your Christian upbringing.'"

Once the pastor more clearly understood the dynamics at work, how was he to deal with the mess he'd created? There were several tempting ways to avoid the issue, he said. One was to return to the keyboard and defend his original position: "You misunderstood me; I'm really a good guy." Another was to dismiss the family, at least emotionally, and encourage them to find another church more consistent with their worldview. Yet another temptation was to apologize and take the blame and tell the family they were completely right.

But the situation was a bit more complex than any of those tempting alternatives would fully address.

"The truth was that in my zeal to engage pop culture, I had become numb to the threat it poses. I needed the reminder—and the humble stick struck me all the harder having been swung by a thirteen-year-old girl.

"But it's also true that our church seeks to live out our core values, one of which is culture-friendliness. We believe glimpses of God can be found in culture, even those parts that are seemingly opposed to him. We envision God as similar to a great judo master, one who uses the opponent's energy to his own advantage. Hollywood movies and pop songs reveal God even in their opposition to him, and often they tell the human story such that our need for God comes through loud and clear. Though I'd promoted this conviction with a poor attitude and failed to employ it appropriately, I could not toss it away just to salve this conflict. But this was clearly too much to put into an email."

So he wrote back to the girl and her mother: "I came across as a jerk because I can be one, and because I wasn't careful with my attitude and words. Can we get together and talk?"

A couple days later, the pastor met with the family. He apologized for his hasty and cavalier email. Then he asked the girl what she felt when she heard him mention the *Matrix* movies in the sermon and what concerns that raised for her.

He listened. Along the way he affirmed her desire to live with a pure heart and to keep the values of God's kingdom front and center. When she and her mother had both been heard, he talked about his desire, and the church's core values, to love God and to reach people who are caught up in the world's culture. He said that how those two commandments are lived out, at the same time, often causes disagreements among Christians.

"I told the family that lovers of Christ could disagree on these things and asked them to respect my conviction as I would respect theirs. I also gave the family my permission to seek a new community of faith since I'd given them reason not to respect me.

"Surprisingly, they refused. They apologized for being quick to judge me, and they asked my forgiveness and said they would remain in the church if it was okay with me.

"I repeated my apology and replied that the next time we met I would be the first to say, 'I love you guys.' Email alone does not suffice in complex dynamics like this. Sometimes words have to be spoken that the people we love can hear.

"We exchanged apologies, hugged, and ended up laughing at ourselves. They remain active in the church and serve to remind me of my need to avoid cultural compromise as well as self-centeredness."

Why E-communication Heightens Conflict

As these accounts demonstrate, electronic communication can have unintended consequences. It has a natural tendency to escalate conflict. It requires intentional effort in email to de-escalate tensions. Why is that?

According to a study by Raymond Friedman and Steven Currall,[2] some of the benefits of email can also increase conflict.

- Email is an isolated activity. You don't need anyone around to read or respond to email. This makes it convenient. But it also means you miss all the nonverbal cues: vocal inflections, facial expressions, gestures. So it's easy to overlook the actual person we're emailing, which means that misunderstandings are more likely to arise.

- Email doesn't convey context. We experience email as words on a screen, but we miss seeing a unique face in a unique context. One report on this study concludes: "This makes it easy to forget the humanness of our recipient. Consequently, email style tends to be more serious and less friendly, more aggressive and less polite."[3]

It helps to remember that in face-to-face communication there are three elements that combine to get the message across. They are, in order of importance: (1) body language, (2) tone of voice, (3) words. The nonverbal elements are particularly important for communicating feelings and attitude, especially in situations when there is tension. And if words and body language disagree, one tends to believe the body language.

In email, we must overcompensate with our words to make up for the lack of the other two elements of communication. Here are some ways to do that.

Whenever there is conflict, you should use email:

- If there needs to be a record of the interaction.
- If you are dealing with a conflict where the emotional level is fairly low.
- If you can be gracious and not upset as you're drafting your reply.
- If you are having an initial conversation to set up a phone call or a face-to-face meeting to address things in more detail.

Do not use email:

- If you're in conflict with someone you've never met face-to-face.
- If your emotions are running high.
- If the email exchange has gone back and forth more than three times. This could mean that the issue is too complex to deal with using only email. Ask to speak by phone or face-to-face.

If you absolutely must deal with detailed conflict by email, because of space or time issues, here are some reminders:

1. When creating an email in a conflicted situation, insert the address last. Too many emails have been sent inadvertently before they were ready.

2. Don't assume why a person didn't respond to an email or answered your email in a certain manner. Intentions are invisible. Get more information, or give the person every benefit of the doubt.

3. Remind yourself of the importance of your relationship with the other party. Include in your message reminders of this relationship. Communicate your desire for the other person's best interests.

4. Avoid being hyper-rational. Don't try to parse the words the other person used and dissect the word choices. Remember that differences are resolved with healthy emotion and relationships—not just logic.

5. Beware of perceived insults that you never intended. Go the extra mile to be respectful and gracious. When the other party sees only your words on a screen, without facial expressions, body language, or social cues, it's easy to misunderstand and misinterpret words.

6. Remember that your responses can also be interpreted as being more aggressive than intended. Reread them before sending and anticipate your reader's worst possible reaction. Don't use barbed words that carry emotion beyond their meaning. Be sure to communicate your spirit, not just your position on the issues at hand.

7. Think before you hit the send button. If you're unsure, give it some time in your draft box, or email it to yourself for further review. Hit send only when you're satisfied that this email will help, not worsen, the conflict.

8. Be careful with "cc's" and the message they send. This may imply that you are ratting a person out to other friends or colleagues.

One church leader in Indiana, Angie Ward, came to several conclusions as a result of some unfortunate experiences with electronic communications and conflict.

"Our church is tech-savvy," Angie said. "We use email regularly for announcements, prayer updates, and notes between staff. But one thing we no longer do with email is handle conflict. We learned the hard way. Email and texting are not suited for dealing with conflict.

"First, email and texting are easily misunderstood. Readings of emotional tone are often wrong. People read into things what they think you feel. During one heart-to-heart online conversation, being a fast typist, I responded quickly to each of my friend's posts. I noticed she became defensive and the conversation ended. It was weeks before I learned that she had been offended by the speed of my replies. She interpreted my rapid posts to mean I was angry. After making peace, we agreed to talk in person next time.

"Second, email and texting are part of a read-and-reply culture. If you are angry, it's all too easy to 'vent and send' before considering all the facts. Last year, one of our volunteers heard about a budget issue that made him angry. He immediately fired off a harshly critical missive regarding the church's leadership. While every member has a right to raise questions, his email was inflammatory and based on misinformation. Checking the facts beforehand would have kept his message out of the 'outgoing' folder.

"Third, online conflict spreads like wildfire. It's too easy to forward email to lots of people, many of whom may not need to get involved. Add to this the varying frequency that people check email, and soon no one knows who has seen what, which only adds more fuel to the fire.

"I was surprised one Sunday morning to learn of a heated, critical email generated by a key leader. I was even more shocked to learn who had received it. Current leadership, past leadership, and others who were completely uninvolved in the issues—all were blind copied.

"Fortunately, the situation was contained and the author issued a personal apology to the entire distribution list—but only after a face-to-face visit from the pastor. Some things are best handled in person.

"Now, when an incendiary email or text comes to me, I fire off an automatic reply, but with an invitation: 'I'd be happy to get together with you to talk about this issue. Give me a call, and let's set up a time.'"

5

When the Mind Isn't Quite Right

Discernment is not a matter of simply telling the difference between right and wrong; rather it is telling the difference between right and almost right.

Charles Haddon Spurgeon

The worship team was making its way off the stage, and Pastor Mike was making his way up, when he noticed movement off to the side of the auditorium. A woman he had never seen before, with flaming red hair, suddenly stood to her feet, eyes shut, face to the sky, hands in the air. At the top of her lungs, she started uttering unintelligible syllables: "Ah, shalamakea lohiritu. Gristomay tomballo. Lavamar formallat sisternia."

The whole church was shocked into complete silence. Pastor Mike was as stunned as everyone else.

"This was a 135-year-old Baptist church where this sort of thing had never been done," Mike said later. "Other than the woman belting it out, you could have heard a pin drop. The look on most of the faces of the congregation was pure terror. A few were looking at me as if they thought this was something staged for effect, a creative sermon intro. But it wasn't.

"As the woman continued, everyone looked at me, their eyes wide. They seemed to be pleading with me, 'Do something! What are you going to do about this?' The truth is, I had no idea. Nothing like this had been covered in seminary or ministry conferences. And I'd not been in churches where these sorts of utterances were practiced."

Saying a silent prayer, Mike slowly walked over to the woman, as attentive as possible to what was happening. With her eyes closed, the woman didn't see him coming.

When he got to her, Mike gently laid his hand on her shoulder to let her know that he was there.

With that, she switched and began to speak in English, but still with a voice that carried to every corner of the room: "I am the Alpha and the Omega, the beginning and the end, the Ancient of Days, the Lion of Judah. I have created the world, the firmament above and the earth below. Mighty are the works of my hands, and marvelous is that which is made, great in glory and in majesty."

Although her presentation was disruptive, Mike didn't hear her saying anything that was irrational or unbiblical, so he simply let her continue for a moment or two ("although it seemed like an aching eternity," Mike said). As he watched her speak, he noticed that sitting next to her was a man who seemed very uncomfortable, who was touching her arm trying to coax her down.

At that point, the woman said, "I love my daughter with a great love, and though she has been in mental hospitals, even now my favor rests upon her. . . ."

Mike bent down to quietly ask the man, "Is she speaking about herself right now?" The man nodded. So Mike asked, "What is her name?" He responded, "Darlene."

"At that moment I felt like I had my first clue what was happening here," Mike said later.

With that, Pastor Mike turned to the rapt faces in the congregation and with the benefit of the microphone said gently, "Church, this is Darlene, and she is our guest today. I think that we should pause right now to pray for her."

While Mike prayed, with his hand gently on her shoulder, Darlene continued speaking forcefully. Mike asked that God would touch Darlene in a special way, bringing comfort to her mind, clarity to her thoughts, and calmness to her soul. And that God's Holy Spirit, the spirit of peace, *shalom,* would be evident in her life. As he finished praying, to everyone's surprise and relief, Darlene also brought her prophecy to a close.

Mike described it later with a grin: "As I said Amen, she sat back down and rejoined the service already in progress."

Even though he doubted anyone would remember anything he had to say that morning in his sermon on Ephesians chapter 1, it seemed essential to press forward and reestablish a sense of normalcy.

At the end of the service, Darlene and her companion exited immediately, before Mike or anyone else could talk with them.

With the benediction, the immediate feeling in the room was one of relief. Everyone wore nervous smiles.

"I usually don't walk out of worship just grateful to be alive, but I am today," one woman told Mike.

But a number of people made a point of telling Mike that they appreciated that he had treated Darlene with compassion and humanity. "We could have taken the service back lots of different ways," Mike said, "but the Lord enabled us to find one that treated her with honor as a person."

That week, after a few phone calls, Mike learned that Darlene had a treatable mental condition but she had gone off her medication, and that had prompted her behavior on that Sunday morning. Darlene left Mike a phone message a couple of weeks later from a nearby mental health treatment facility.

"Knowing her situation enabled us to respond with greater understanding," Mike said.

How Widespread Is This?

Public disturbances such as this are relatively rare, but other less dramatic encounters with mental illness in the church are increasingly common. In fact, mental disorders are the number-one cause of disability in North America. Some of the most common are mood disorders, depression, autism, and attention deficit disorder.

According to the National Institute of Mental Health, more than 25 percent of Americans ages 18 and older suffer from a diagnosable mental disorder in a given year.[1] "That's about equal to the total percentage of people diagnosed with

cancer each year, those living with heart disease, those in-
fected with HIV and AIDS and those afflicted with diabetes—
combined,"[2] according to Amy Simpson, author of *Troubled
Minds: Mental Illness and the Church's Mission*. She says that

> because many mental illnesses (like depressive episodes) are
> short-term and not chronic, a higher percentage of people
> are affected by a mental illness at some time in their lives.
>
> Serious and chronic mental illness is less common, but
> still present among 6 percent of the population, or one in
> seventeen adults. . . . Those mental illnesses considered "seri-
> ous" are major depression, schizophrenia, bipolar disorder,
> obsessive-compulsive disorder (OCD), panic disorder, post-
> traumatic stress disorder (PTSD), and borderline personality
> disorder. . . .
>
> Nearly everyone is touched by mental illness—directly or
> indirectly—at some point. . . . If your church is typical of
> the US population, on any given Sunday one in four adults
> and one in five children sitting around you are suffering from
> a mental illness. Many of them are under the influence of
> powerful antipsychotic drugs and their side effects.[3]

In partnership with *Leadership Journal,* Amy Simpson
recently conducted a survey of five hundred churches, using
the National Alliance on Mental Illness definition of mental
illness: "a medical condition that disrupts a person's thinking,
feeling, mood, ability to relate to others and daily function-
ing" and "often result[s] in a diminished capacity for coping
with the ordinary demands of life."[4] In this survey, 98 percent of respondents (all pastors and other church leaders)
indicated they were aware of mental illnesses or disorders
among people in their congregations.[5] Indeed, 37 percent

indicated that someone in their congregation had suffered from a psychotic disorder such as schizophrenia.[6]

The mentally ill often feel they are on the margins of society, but they're actually in the mainstream!

And yet the survey also found that only 13 percent of responding church leaders said mental illness is discussed openly and in a healthy way in their churches.[7]

After analyzing the data, Amy Simpson observed, "As we're busy enthusiastically delivering meals to suffering people, we are largely ignoring the afflictions of 25 percent of our population. . . . No wonder several people I talked with called mental illness the 'no-casserole illness.'"[8]

One church leader in North Carolina, who leads a support group ministry to people affected by mental illness, described his church as "large, resourced, and decidedly pain avoidant." In his church, "While great care and effort is taken to organize outreach overseas—and even across town—the closer the pain is to home, the more threatening. The suffering of folks with severe and persistent mental illness and emotional wounds is likely the most threatening of all *because it impacts most of our families.* Families most typically stay quiet, for fear that disclosure will have a chilling effect on their social status and inclusion."

And in that awkward climate of pain and silence, conditions are conducive to surprise appearances of dragon behavior.

In most cases, those with mental illness do not themselves present a direct danger to the church. In the rare cases in which there is a real threat of violence, churches often get a restraining order, which can be enforced by the police.

Most often, those with mental illness complicate church life in other ways. They may indirectly lead to "dragon problems" because people in the church differ dramatically over how much accommodation the church should make for them.

For instance, in one church a girl with a form of autism had a service dog, without which she had difficulty coping in a group setting. Her parents assumed her dog would be welcome in the Sunday school room. Normally that wouldn't have been a problem, except that another child in that Sunday school class had an allergy to dogs. The two mothers, determined to protect the welfare of their children, forced the church to decide between them. Each mother saw it as an "us or them" situation.

If a person with a mental illness has tics or involuntary verbalization, how much tolerance does the church have for distractions in the worship service? Or if a child with mental illness or ADHD wants to dance during the music . . . or if a person with schizophrenia "has something to say," will that be permitted?

Given the pervasive presence of various forms of mental illness, how can church leaders respond in ways that benefit those with mental illness while not derailing the overall ministry of the church?

For the dragons that emerge because of the corollary issues surrounding mental illness, the strategies in the rest of this book apply. But some strategies are appropriate for the situations directly involving those with mental illness.

Pastors who have experience with these situations offer these bits of wisdom they've gained the hard way.

Align Your Attitude

Those with mental illness can seem like "a black hole of pastoral care," as one pastor put it. They can "burn up pastoral fuel and then press harder on the accelerator," wrote another. Other church members may gossip or gripe about them. "Remember, Pastor," a pillar of the church told him, "that element doesn't pay the bills around here."

But the pastors I interviewed resist the temptation to become callous: "I can't imagine Jesus gossiping about that incredibly needy Gerasene demoniac or those ungrateful lepers. Christ accepted them. He touched them. True, Jesus spent only a minority of his time with the chronically needy, but there was space in his schedule for some powerful ministry encounters with them. Jesus never anesthetized his heart to the hurt that surrounded him."

One pastor said: "I try to remember that everyone is bearing a painful soul wound. Consider Joe, who for years struggled with deep-seated transvestitism. Most people couldn't or didn't want to understand Joe's struggles. They never listened long enough to hear the incredible brokenness in Joe's past: two abusive older brothers who ridiculed his masculinity, a needy mother who dressed him in girl's clothing, and a violent father who affirmed only little girls. This doesn't justify any of the sinful choices Joe has made (something he freely acknowledges), but it shows that Joe the very draining person is also Joe the very wounded person."

Prayer is essential in cultivating the right heart. As Dietrich Bonhoeffer wrote, "I can no longer condemn or hate a brother for whom I pray, no matter how much trouble he causes me. His face, that hitherto may have been strange and intolerable to me, is transformed in intercession into the countenance of a brother for whom Christ died, the face of a forgiven sinner."[9]

In the case of mental illness, the key element is to destigmatize the condition. "I try to reduce the stigma by referring to standard mental health issues like depression and addiction in my messages," said one pastor in a college town, where he previously was a college dean. "I use stories I've read involving mental illness as introductions or illustrations. And I try to communicate that mental health issues are not spiritual failings. God heals in many ways, including through carefully regulated doses of mood-stabilizing drugs. And God can use these conditions to draw people closer to himself."

Communicate Clear Boundaries

Boundaries may seem a contradiction to acceptance, but only if we confuse acceptance with availability. They are not the same. Those with mental illness tend to overdose on an unlimited supply of pastoral availability.

When Ed entered a twenty-one-day treatment program for a mood disorder (his fourth treatment program), he told his pastor he needed to talk to him every day. The pastor expressed his concern and promised to pray for him every day, but he told Ed he would not visit him during this inpatient program: "Ed, you are too dependent on others, and I want to give you the space you need to grow strong in God's love."

This may seem blunt, but Ed never grasped all the hints and implied boundaries. Lovingly but firmly, the pastor lowered Ed's expectations of his availability.

This pastor said, "Working with people like Ed has led me to three principles regarding boundary-setting:

"1. I must take the initiative. If I don't, people like Ed will innocently assume total pastoral availability.
"2. Boundaries must be specific, clearly defining when and where I will be available. Vague boundaries don't work.
"3. With love and gentleness, I must verbalize boundaries and then lovingly stand my ground."

John, a troubled twenty-year-old, had a knack for calling his pastor at home during critical family times: supper, bedtime stories, "together time" with his wife. "His timing was uncanny," said the pastor. "It felt as if he had bugged the house. Finally, I set the following boundary: 'I'd love to talk to you, John, but I can't accept calls at home anymore. If you call me at church, I'll give you my full attention.' The calls still came for a while, but I didn't pick up. It was important to stand by my boundary, for my family's sake, and for John's sake."

Boundary setting can feel cold, but it's necessary for pastoral effectiveness. Indeed, for many, loving acceptance with boundaries is what fosters spiritual growth. Henri Nouwen calls this the "ministry of absence." Nouwen continues, "We ministers may have become so available that there is too much presence and too little absence . . . too much of us and too little of God and his Spirit."[10]

"I have sometimes been so available that needy people used me as a substitute high priest," said John's pastor. "Unwittingly, I usurped Christ's role in the sanctification process. By prayerfully limiting my availability, I was encouraging him to stand up straight and receive the healing that only Christ can give."

Pursue Servanthood, Not "Success"

There's a temptation in church ministry to assume that everyone's problem can be solved.

"After renewing his commitment to Christ, one troubled young man vanished, and I heard he'd rejoined the transvestite subculture of Las Vegas," said a pastor in Minnesota. "Roselda, a schizophrenic mother with a young son, started a new wonder drug, regained custody of her son, and even joined our church choir. But within four months, everything unraveled. She left the church, lost her son, and returned to the local psychiatric ward. Before I got here, it never occurred to me that some deeply wounded people might go backward instead of forward."

Ministering to those with mental illness involves the likelihood of apparent failure. We won't help everyone. Some will make visible strides; others will stall or regress. This reality can challenge our notions of ministry. "I prefer—sometimes demand—success. At the least, I want to avoid failure," said a pastor from New York. "So I gravitate toward people who will make me look and feel successful about my ministry. Those with mental illness usually don't qualify as success-enhancers."

They do, however, qualify as servanthood enhancers. Servanthood, not visible success, is our calling. Success is usually about me, my need for approval, and visible results. Servanthood is about God, about "not my will but your will be done." And in that transfer of will, we fulfill our deepest longing to glorify him.

Step After Faithful Step

Let's return to the story that opened this chapter, in which Darlene interrupted the worship service. Pastor Mike took some key steps and learned some ministry-altering lessons.

Knowing that it was up to him, as leader, to guide the church's response, to set the tone, to interpret what had happened, Pastor Mike met on Monday with the church leaders to process the experience, pray, and plan their next steps.

"For better or worse, the church was going to be watching me to keep the peace, set the tone, and interpret what had happened. I knew I needed to do that for the congregation right away—addressing both the personal and theological issues that the Sunday morning experience had raised."

On Tuesday he sent an email to the congregation, mostly to set the tone. "They knew that we had made it through the disruption, the woman had been treated with kindness, and order had been restored—but they also needed to know that I was still smiling. People carefully watch their pastors. Are they worried? Is there something to fear? They needed to be assured that I was confident, faith-filled, and excited to be back with them the next weekend."

In the Tuesday email, Mike wrote, "I heard someone say once that 'If you have the Word without the Spirit you'll dry up. If you have the Spirit without the Word you'll blow up. But if you have the Word and the Spirit, you'll grow up.' I can't wait until next Sunday because we're going to have both the Word and the Spirit."

He said that next Sunday he wanted to share with them some reflections on the unusual circumstances of the week before and some things they all could learn from the experience.

"They needed to hear from me that this was going to end up being a good thing," Mike said.

The next Sunday morning, Darlene was nowhere to be seen. ("But I promise you, we were looking," Mike said.) Attendance was high. People were eager to find out how the church was going to handle what they had been through. Early in the service, Mike took ten minutes or so to have a "fireside chat" with the congregation: "Last week we had a very unusual experience with a visitor in our service, and I just want to reflect with you a little bit about what happened and what we can learn from that."

He shared how important it was that they do everything they could to treat everyone with a sense of respect and humanity, even those who stretched them out of their comfort zones.

"Often we get opportunities during the week to practice that. This past Sunday, we just had an opportunity to all practice it together. And I want you to know how proud I am of you," Mike said. "But it does raise an interesting question: What if God did want to communicate to us something that wasn't on our agenda? Could that happen? And what could we expect if it did?" He talked about the need to keep open the possibility that God might have a word for them that they weren't expecting—and the biblical criteria for evaluating unexpected messages. He closed by reiterating how proud he was of them for acting with such grace.

"One of the key values that we had been focusing on in the church was embracing outsiders," Mike said, reflecting on the situation. "And the church, filled mostly with older, traditional Baptists, had been working hard to reach out and welcome new kinds of attenders—the homeless and poor, ex-cons and drug addicts. We had been learning how it is sometimes too easy to simply serve the needs of outsiders and keep them at arm's length. The real test is how you welcome them into your own community.

"We had been working hard to open our doors wide to the community. Darlene's visit was a watershed moment for us. We needed to see, in real time, how someone would be treated if they didn't exactly fit into our comfort zone. Could we welcome such people, treat them with grace, and still keep the church together and out of chaos? Darlene showed us that we could. It was a turning point, a defining moment."

Then Mike led in a time of prayer. "We prayed for Darlene again and for God's blessing and peace on her life. We prayed for our own hearts, that God would help us to honor people who are beyond our comfort zone. And then we prayed that God would speak to us, and that we would be ready to listen, even if it should come in a way that we weren't expecting."

The congregation responded very positively.

The Surprise (and Secret) Ending

But that's not the end of the story. Several months later, a very quiet woman with dark brown hair came up to Pastor Mike after the service with her Bible in hand. She seemed very shy, and she thanked him for the service.

After a pause she said, "You don't remember me, do you?"

"I'm sorry," Mike said. "I don't think I do. How do we know each other?"

"The last time I was here, I stood up in the service to say something," she said.

"You're Darlene?" Mike said, astonished. He would never have recognized her. Gone was the flaming red hair. Gone was the loud voice. She was so transformed.

"Yes," she replied bashfully. "That's me. But I don't want people to think of me the way I was the last time I was here."

Mike gave her a warm hug and welcomed her back. For the next several years, until she moved to Idaho, she was a part of the church, faithful every Sunday and even helping with community service projects.

"Although Darlene became a part of the congregation, I never pointed out who she was," Mike said. "No one recognized her, and she never brought it up with anyone else. It was obvious that God was working in her life. But I wasn't going to reveal Darlene's past connection with our church. That was a story she could tell if she wanted to, but it wasn't my place to draw attention to that part of her life.

"To this day, almost no one in the church has realized that quiet, meek Darlene was the same wild-eyed prophet from that unforgettable Sunday. No one who was there that Sunday will ever forget it. But as brown-haired Darlene quietly slipped into the life of our church, the congregation embraced the fiery-haired prophet into their lives, more than they ever could have known."

6

The Play for Power

To see that my adversary gives me my rights is natural; but . . .
from our Lord's standpoint it does not matter if I am de-
frauded or not; what does matter is that I do not defraud.

Oswald Chambers

You may be able to compel people to maintain certain mini-
mum standards by stressing duty, but the highest moral and
spiritual achievements depend not upon a push but a pull.
People must be charmed into righteousness.

Reinhold Niebuhr

Not all attacks by dragons are personal or electronic or influ-
enced by mental issues; sometimes the play is for power, pure
and simple. People use power tactics to influence decisions
such as getting the church involved in a particular political

cause, or focusing on a particular form of Bible study rather than outreach, or spending money on mission trips rather than facilities.

Well-intentioned dragons, of course, have good reasons for seeking power, for swaying votes, for pressuring leaders—usually because the church is heading in a direction they think needs to be changed. When two groups differ over the goals and direction of the church, tensions naturally rise as they each try to gain the upper hand. If the issues are significant, both sides know the consequences of losing—the church won't be the same again. All the ingredients are there for a firefight . . . with all the resulting casualties.

Even the New Testament church knew the pain of living as a house divided until some key issues were settled.

In Galatians 2, Paul describes his own power struggle with some "false believers" (v. 4) over the expectations placed on Gentiles who were converting to Christianity. His opponents, known as the circumcision party, demanded that new Christians be circumcised and meet Jewish lifestyle requirements before joining the Christian church. Paul refused to bow to that position, insisting that faith is the only prerequisite.

Paul and Barnabas brought Titus, an uncircumcised Greek convert, to Jerusalem to force the issue, and the church leaders—Peter, James, and John—accepted him. They also offered Paul and Barnabas the "right hand of fellowship" (v. 9), confirming the validity of their work with Gentiles.

This did not, however, solve the power struggle. The circumcision party was still strong enough to eventually sway Peter. Earlier, Peter had spoken out against partiality when Cornelius, a Roman centurion, had become a believer. But when Peter visited Antioch, he bowed to pressure from the hard core and avoided eating with the Gentiles. Paul confronted Peter publicly for his inconsistency, and while Peter's response isn't recorded, Paul apparently was vindicated (vv. 11–21).

But still the power struggle raged. Paul and Barnabas got into a "sharp dispute and debate" with their opponents (Acts 15:2), and knowing Paul as we do from the rest of the New Testament, that's probably putting it mildly. Paul wrote an entire letter to the Galatians attacking his opponents, whom he branded "accursed" (Galatians 1:8–9 KJV).

A council in Jerusalem was called to rule on the question.

It was theological, emotional, and ecclesiastical hardball. When the clash was over, the church was split, the winners—Paul, Peter, Barnabas, and Silas—going on to take the lead, write the New Testament, and turn an empire upside down. The losers faded into history, nameless characters known only as Judaizers.

The character of the church was forever changed because of the outcome. The power struggle ended, we now agree, with the right side on top. The essence of the gospel was at stake. Wouldn't it have been different, and tragic, if the wrong group had won?

Later church wars were fought over the writings to be included in the canon, the language used to describe the nature of Jesus, and the relationship of Father, Son, and Holy Spirit.

Yes, some power plays have to be made; some wars have to be fought—and won.

Churches today have power struggles just as brutal. Most of them deal with matters of practice, not belief, but the hostilities aroused are as heated as if the essence of the gospel were at stake. The choir, for instance, has often been branded the War Department of the church. The Battle of the Budget can rival the Battle of the Bulge as different ministries vie for funding. One church nearly split over whether to accept and use a wealthy member's estate gift of real estate or sell it and give the money to the poor.

These can be significant issues. But worth fighting for? Worth damaging friendships over? Worth splitting a church for?

How much firepower is appropriate in a church fight? No Geneva Convention has established any rules.

The problem is that most church members imagine themselves as basically "nice," willing to bend to keep the peace. This gives lots of leverage, sometimes complete control, to those hard-nosed individuals willing to make a public scene. Out of a desire to keep the peace, many in the congregation will give them extra space, which translates into power—power to veto programs, to overrule pastors, to alter the direction of the church. Churches can thus be victimized by people who see being "right" as more important than being "nice." Those who make absolutes out of issues others see as negotiable can stymie the will of the majority. Unless the church has an unusually effective board, this usually means the pastor has to fight the battle or else abandon the field to the dragon's faction.

A healthy congregation doesn't allow one or two members to set the church's direction or change its mission. Neither does it have to enter into open warfare. Sometimes the answer is being nice . . . and firm.

"But the Future Is at Stake"

Charles Westerman was surprised when Jack Kenton was picked by the nominating committee for the position of board chairman. Only six months earlier, Charles had heard via the grapevine that Jack's family was thinking of leaving Morningside Chapel. Charles remembered several occasions when Jack had said to him, "Pastor, the church isn't as friendly as it used to be; we're growing too fast to keep up with everyone."

That wasn't an unusual observation, and Charles agreed but said he guessed it was a nice problem to have. The church, just outside Harrisburg, Pennsylvania, had grown from eight hundred to fifteen hundred members in the last three years. Lots of people drifted in and stayed, happy with the strong music program and Charles's clear and powerful preaching; others drifted off, blaming the church's size for an impersonal feel. Charles felt he was doing what he could to foster intimacy through adult "life groups," but he recognized that large churches would naturally feel different than small ones.

Jack, a fifty-five-year-old executive, hadn't been very active for the past year, but suddenly he was the nominee for the board chairmanship. One of Jack's closest friends, Chris Porter, was chairman of the nominating committee, and Judy Kenton, Jack's wife, was also on the committee. The Porters and the Kentons were among the "old guard" that had been in the church for years. They'd apparently convinced a majority of the twelve-member committee that Jack would do a good job.

When he first heard about the nomination, Charles spoke with Chris Porter.

"I've worked with two board chairmen in the six years I've been here," said Charles. "And I had a close relationship with both of them. I've had lunch once or twice with Jack, and we're not particularly close. I'm not sure we see eye to eye on a number of things. I'd prefer another candidate."

"Jack's a good man, Pastor," Chris said. "He's a spiritual leader in his home, he's a student of Scripture, and he's memorized more verses than most people have read. He knows our church and its needs. I think he'll work well with the board. Besides, he's already accepted the nomination. If we take his name out of the running, he'll know someone objected, and he'll probably leave the church."

Charles suspected Chris would tell Jack who the "someone" was. In fact, he suspected a bit of a power play—an attempt by the old guard to limit his leadership, to put the brakes on the church's growth, to move the attention away from attracting new people and back to the core group.

He didn't want to alienate the charter members of the church. They were an important part of the flock and deserved to be heard. Many of the newcomers could be transferred back to Ohio or New York in a year or two, and the old guard would still be there. But Charles felt part of the church's mission was to continually reach out and to make the church as accessible to newcomers as possible. Jack would undoubtedly resist that.

On the other hand, Charles didn't want to veto the twelve members of the nominating committee, six of whom were board members; he honestly didn't want to stack the board, and he didn't want to be accused of running a dictatorship. After all, he was pleased with the rest of the slate of officers. Why be picky over one nomination?

So he committed himself to serving with Jack and making him a successful board chairman. From the pulpit, Charles thanked the nominating committee for their "strong choices" and watched as the entire slate was unanimously voted in.

A breakfast meeting with Jack seemed to go reasonably well, both men agreeing to work together and Jack quoting his verse of the week, Psalm 26:8—"Lord, I have loved the habitation of thy house, and the place where thine honour dwelleth" (KJV)—but Charles was slightly uncomfortable with Jack's tone.

"He's playing a game of spiritual one-upsmanship, at least that's how it feels," Charles confided to his wife. "He said he hoped he could help bring more depth to our ministry. He said he'd be praying for revival in my life and the lives of our staff. You can't argue with that, but he definitely puts you on the defensive."

Despite their promise to work together, Charles and Jack were butting heads from the first board meeting. Jack questioned the pastor's upcoming sermon series as "pandering to the market rather than opening the Word." The entire board was in turmoil, the air thick with tension and distrust. Jack had a way of questioning motives and intentions. Most of the issues had to do with expansion and growth.

"Are you sure you're not just trying to build an empire?" he asked Charles more than once. Charles didn't know how to respond. "No, I don't want an empire, Jack," he said. "Neither do I want to limit what the Spirit can do." But Jack continued voicing his suspicions. Anything that might suggest further enlargement—renting space for a growing youth ministry, new support groups, rearranging the offices, hiring a part-time bookkeeper—Jack was against.

"Why should we be trying to get more people when we're not doing that great a job with those we've already got?" he asked.

He vehemently opposed a plan to research a possible relocation to a site where the church could construct a larger building. He persuaded a majority of the board, and the plan was defeated. He refused to take part in selecting an architect to draw up plans for possibly enlarging the existing facility. When the vote to approve the architect's proposal came to the board, as chair he made sure everyone knew he did not approve, but the board voted 11–1 to proceed.

That was the first of many 11–1 votes. Even though Jack was outnumbered, his Luddite assaults often caused the board to delay votes, hoping to reach consensus. It rarely did. But action was bogged down for weeks.

Charles continued to meet with Jack once a month for breakfast. Jack complained, "You and the board aren't in submission to me. I've been elected chairman, placed in spiritual authority over this church, and you're resisting my leadership."

"Jack, there's got to be mutual submission," Charles said. "I must submit to the elders, but we must work together, trying to see the full picture, including other points of view."

"Well, I don't like the way you make unilateral decisions," Jack continued. "I hear you're going to California in July to speak at Mount Hermon for a week. You never cleared that with me. You need to run these things by me."

"I don't work for you," Charles said. "I don't even work *for* Morningside Chapel. I work *with* Morningside Chapel.

I'm self-employed—look at my IRS form! I submit myself to the board of elders and the church, but I'm not an employee. I'm an ordained minister, charged with shepherding this flock. Some of these personal ministry decisions are mine."

Jack wouldn't buy it. "I think you have a spiritual problem, Charles. I don't think you're the man for this church. If you had the gift of discernment, you could see that this church needs more depth, needs discipleship, needs revival. Have you been praying for revival in your own life?"

"Yes, I have been . . . daily." *Actually*, Charles thought, *I should have said nightly*. Most nights he had been waking up at 2 a.m.—tossing and turning till 4 or 5—praying and worrying about the direction of the church, asking God to show him any ways to resolve the tensions, trying to think of any new angles he hadn't seen yet. Was there really a growing dissatisfaction, or was he just more aware of it because of Jack's constant harping? Was the church growing too fast? If people kept coming, what alternative was there other than welcoming them and trying to minister to them all?

Is Jack right about my motives? Charles would ask himself night after night. *I don't think so, but how can anyone know for sure? Of course, my ego feels better when the church is growing, but above all else I can honestly say my greatest desire is that God be honored by what we do here.*

Charles continued to lose sleep, but he didn't know how to work with Jack. The monthly breakfasts were becoming an ordeal. Jack's persistent charge was that Charles wasn't spiritual enough to lead a church the size of Morningside. Bickering about spirituality, Charles concluded, is the most perverse kind of bickering.

Eventually, Charles told two of the elders about his deteriorating relationship with Jack. "We're like a husband and wife who bicker not only over the way the house is kept but whether the other partner is fit company," he said. "There's no way a marriage can last if that keeps up. We've been stymied as a church, the Spirit is gone from our board meetings, and we aren't acting in one accord. Eleven-to-one votes are becoming a Monday night liturgy. We're spinning our wheels. Am I the cause of the discord? Maybe if I resigned, the church would become more united."

The two elders said no, they didn't see the situation as that serious. "Eleven to one doesn't bother us, Pastor. And I'm sure you and Jack will eventually work things out. You just see things differently." Charles realized none of the board had heard Jack's private tirades. While he laid into Charles at the breakfasts, Jack's board meeting criticisms were more general, less pointed, and only Charles felt their full impact because he knew what was behind them.

Charles could not tell how many others in the congregation Jack represented. At the breakfasts, Jack kept bringing up names of people he'd been talking to, and to hear him tell it, half the church was disgruntled.

The tensions not only cost Charles sleep, but they also led to some errors of judgment.

"One Sunday I preached from 1 Corinthians 1:10 about 'Them,' those people in our lives who cause confusion and discord, especially in the church," Charles remembers. "I could tell by people's expressions that I'd completely lost them. Afterward my wife said, 'I think I know what you were saying, but I'm sure no one else did.' She was right. It was an oblique sermon, preached out of my own frustration, but the congregation wondered, *What in the world is he talking about?* They thought everything in the church was going fine."

One Sunday in September, just after school started, the sanctuary was packed for both services, and people were sitting in folding chairs in the aisles. Charles asked all the members of Morningside to stand up. "Look around, and see how crowded we are," he instructed. "Now you know why we're considering enlarging our sanctuary." With nervous laughter, people sat back down.

"It was tasteless," Charles now admits. "It was not something I should have done. It was driving a thumbtack home with a sledgehammer to try to make a point with a very small faction. I did it out of frustration, knowing we had to grow but very aware of the people opposed to growth."

In November, six months after Jack had taken office, the hostilities escalated. Early one Thursday morning, Charles was sitting in the restaurant, waiting for Jack to arrive. He was sipping coffee over the sports page when Jack tapped him on the shoulder. "Can I see you outside?" he asked.

Strange request, Charles thought as he followed Jack outside. *He's a busy man, but if he can't stay for breakfast today, why didn't he call or just say so at the table?*

Once outside, however, Jack angrily turned on the pastor. "I've lost all respect for you, Charles. You're no spiritual leader, and I don't think I can even talk with you anymore. It's a waste of time for us to keep meeting for breakfast. We don't get anything accomplished because you don't understand what the people need."

Charles was stunned but managed to say, "Maybe you're right, Jack. I've thought for some time now that we needed to take this matter of my leadership to the board and let them decide."

"If you do that, I'll resign, and the whole church will know you forced me out." Jack turned, got into his car, and drove off. Charles was left standing alone. *This is ridiculous,* he thought. *We're arguing about who's more spiritual, and we can't act like Christians and share a meal together.*

Should he take this to the board? No, he decided, he didn't want to call Jack's bluff. If he forced the board to decide between him and Jack, he was pretty sure the board would side with him, but it would be ugly. Who knows how many of the old guard would follow Jack out the door, and who knows who would believe the nasty accusations he was sure they'd make to other members of the church?

Without any ideas of positive action to take, he finally decided to do nothing. He prayed for a miracle of reconciliation.

At the previous board meeting, in one of their few unanimous votes, the board had decided to ask for the resignation of the church's youth pastor. Charles agreed with the decision. Eric Runyon simply wasn't a youth pastor. The high schoolers were not attracted to him—with 150 names on the roll, Sunday school attendance dwindled from 75 to 40, and the Wednesday night youth group attracted 30. Eric's wife resented his being out evenings or off on weekend retreats, and he was discovering youth ministry can't be done nine to five. Even Jack had said, "We need to let this young man know that he's really choosing the wrong career."

As distasteful as any firing is, Charles was relieved that at least he and Jack finally agreed on something. The Christian education board had approved the action, Charles had received Eric's resignation, the situation had been explained to the staff, and Charles was confident that all the proper procedures had been followed.

Now the board had to decide how to announce it to the congregation. They felt a brief announcement from the pulpit wasn't adequate. By consensus, the board decided a meeting on a Sunday evening should be held with those most affected—the high schoolers and their parents—to explain the situation. Charles was designated to make the explanation.

That night two hundred teens and parents crowded into the chapel to hear what the pastor had to say. Eric hadn't been able to attract many high schoolers, but when he was let go, several people had been grumbling about the abruptness of it all. Charles hoped he could bring calm.

After explaining that Eric's gifts were in other areas, that the church wished him well as he sought the Lord's direction for his life, and that he would be paid for the rest of the school year, Charles asked if there were any questions or comments.

Immediately Jack stood up. "Yes, I'd like to ask a question."

Charles wondered what he didn't already know about the situation.

"I think you presented only part of the truth about Eric's situation," Jack began. Charles felt anger begin to rise at the accusation. Was Jack calling him a liar?

"Isn't it true that Eric was let go because he wasn't attracting enough kids? It seems to me he was trying to run a quality program for the few. He was at my house last week, and we had a small group over to pray for him, and he told me the goals he'd had for the group. He had a core of thirty on Wednesday nights. You can't develop a huge following in just a year and a half, nor perhaps should you. Isn't it better to build solid ministry with thirty kids rather than chase after a hundred on the fringe?"

While Jack was making his speech, Charles was feeling his temperature rise. *Why is Jack pretending he wasn't in on the decision to let Eric go? What's he trying to do? Embarrass me? Start a mutiny? He's publicly contradicting me.* The hostility that had been building up for six months suddenly exploded.

"All right, Jack, you win. Farewell, friend," Charles said bitterly and walked from the room, slamming the door and leaving the teens and parents speechless. As far as he was concerned, he had quit Morningside Chapel. He was fed up, tired of the battle. Let someone else knock himself silly against this brick wall.

No sooner had he gotten home than Dan Moran, his associate pastor, and two of the board members knocked on the door wanting to know what was going on. They were confused. They had talked with Jack after the meeting, and he was calling for the pastor's resignation. "If the pastor doesn't exercise any more self-control than that, he doesn't have the spiritual qualifications necessary to lead us," he had said. The elders said they were having an emergency meeting the next night to discuss the situation, and they wanted to have all the facts.

Charles explained the whole story, beginning with the discomfort at the nomination, the early tensions, the ongoing inability to find common ground, his difficulty sleeping, the blowup at breakfast, everything.

"I guess we made a mistake agreeing to the meeting with the parents tonight. You don't explain a firing publicly; you make the decision, take the heat, and let it pass," he concluded. "But tonight isn't the real issue. The real issue is the direction of this church—are we going to reach out and continue to grow, or are we going to shut down our growth to concentrate on those we've already got?"

The whole board, minus Jack, met with Charles on Tuesday night. On Thursday night, minus Charles, they met with Jack. On Friday night, the board met with both of them. Jack raised the issue of authority. They discussed what it meant to be in submission to one another. The authority of the chairman, the authority of the board, the authority of the pastor were argued, and delineations were made. After two hours, Charles agreed to submit to the authority of the board as a whole, and Jack agreed that the chairman was "first among equals" on the board and that he, too, would submit to the authority of the board as a whole.

But Saturday morning, Jack changed his mind. He called Charles, said the situation was intolerable, and that he was resigning. Charles said, "I'm sorry you feel that way" but didn't try to change his mind. A congregational meeting was announced for Sunday night.

"I did not appear in the pulpit on Sunday morning," Charles recalls. "I had really blown my cool the previous Sunday night, so I went to the high school class and apologized. I did not use the name of our chairman, but I explained that frustrations in the ministry had been building up and that night they boiled over. I let them know I had acted badly and I was sorry."

Sunday night, the church was packed for the congregational meeting. Rumors and questions had been circulating: Was the pastor resigning? Had the elders fired him? What was happening?

When the chairman's resignation was read, the crowd was silent, but the more perceptive ones knew a power play had been attempted and failed. The vote to accept the resignation was overwhelming: 498–12.

The Kentons and the Porters both stopped attending the church, but most of the old guard stayed. In the months following, 90 percent of the congregation approved expansion issues, but the other 10 percent, while complaining, did not leave the church. Today, people continue to debate ways to make such a large church personal, but the ministry continues to grow. The old guard is no longer making a habit of threatening to leave.

"I was fortunate," Charles concludes. "I made some tactical errors and bad judgments, but I survived because our staff was well liked and our vision for the church was generally accepted. But if Jack Kenton had been able to gain more of a following, he could have split the church."

Reflections From the War Room

What is to be learned from the power struggles in this story and the multiplied thousands of others that could be told? Pastors who have won, and those who have lost, agree on several key principles.

Face into the wind. Boat captains in a storm know that running before the gale can force them onto the rocks. The best chance for surviving the squall of a power play is facing it directly.

Charles Westerman let himself be tossed by the wind, and his frustration built to the point of losing emotional control, almost landing him on the rocks.

"Someone once said, 'Never let your enemy choose the battlefield,'" he reflects. "I don't consider Jack Kenton an enemy, but I certainly let him choose the battlefield. I lost control. If necessary, I should have offered my resignation before the board, not before two hundred people already upset over the youth pastor.

"I should have taken our disagreement to the board from the beginning, certainly at the point when he refused to have breakfast with me," he says. "They could have helped me gauge the strength of the opposition, instead of my losing sleep wondering. If I was out of line, they could have corrected me. If he was wrong, they could have stepped in sooner."

Prevent church fights from becoming holy wars. Nothing is bloodier than a religious war. Issues aren't just seen as human squabbles; everything is elevated to eternal importance. How easy to forget that it was the devil whose tactic in Genesis 3 was getting two people to believe, "You will be like God, knowing good and evil" (v. 5). How tempting even today to mistake our will for God's. How devilish to believe that disagreeing with me is disagreeing with God.

Despite the pop spirituality that says, "Every problem is a spiritual problem," not every disagreement is a clash between good and evil, between the divine and the demonic.

"I wish my church members could recognize that they're just having a barroom scrap," says a Bible church pastor.

123

"Some people enjoy going out on Friday night and getting in a fight with the good ol' boys. You mix it up a while, but nobody holds it against anybody. But in the church, people have to justify their scraps, so they're determined to cast them as the spiritual versus the unspiritual."

Not all problems are spiritual problems. Some are personality differences, some differing philosophies of ministry, some just a dogged desire to disagree. If people can be given permission to disagree without having their sanctification called into question, church fights won't be so bloody.

One Massachusetts pastor had just seen his church break ground for a new sanctuary, but the battle to get the congregation's approval had been costly, and the funding was going to continue to be a struggle. The next day he was in the hospital having X rays for severe stomach pain. His youth pastor came to his bedside.

"I know what's bothering your stomach," the associate said, pausing and looking out the window. "You know, Pastor, this building isn't the greatest thing that's going to happen for the kingdom of God in Massachusetts this week."

"I needed that," the pastor said after his release. "The X rays didn't show a thing, but Rob touched the problem directly. I realized our million-dollar building wouldn't bring God's kingdom one inch closer. He might choose to honor it, but the fact is he doesn't need it, nor does he need any of our self-important efforts."

The pastor's stomach pain disappeared and has not returned.

Learn what you can from the opposition. Power struggles make you do your homework, forcing you to cover every angle, anticipate every criticism, and go by the book.

During a tussle over remodeling the education facility, one pastor learned more about preschoolers' developmental characteristics and square-footage requirements than he ever wanted to know because he knew the opposition would bring those things up in the public meetings. Now he is glad he had to learn those things, since his own children are preschoolers.

During World War II, General Dwight Eisenhower reportedly would not make a tactical decision until he found someone who strongly opposed it. He wanted to see any weaknesses before proceeding. Some pastors have discovered that policy works in the church, too.

"I'm a better administrator because of the difficult people in my church," says a Congregational pastor. "In one case they prevented me from hiring a staff member I really wanted. I eventually discovered they had been right about his weaknesses. In another case, their criticisms of our building plans prepared me for the town council's questions. They made me do my homework, which kept me from looking like an idiot before the community."

Remember that failure is not fatal. Even if the worst happens, a power play succeeds, and a pastor is compelled to concede, whether out of frustration or the efforts of the opposition, that doesn't mean the ministry is over. Even if you are fired or have to resign, the story is not over. Just as one dragon is not the entire church (though at times the angry voices are deafening), so one pastorate is not an entire ministry. Winston Churchill once said, "Success is not final; failure is not fatal; it is the courage to continue that counts."

Pastors who survive the dragon wars unscathed are a small

minority; those who have left a church under less than happy circumstances are legion.

"When I was about to be forced out of my church," says a Kansas pastor, "I was feeling sorry for myself until I talked with an old veteran missionary who was visiting our church. I told him my troubles, and he said, 'Phil, better men than you have been kicked out of a church. It's not the end of the world.' That was just what I needed." That pastor, at fifty-eight years old, is now happily ministering in another, though smaller, congregation.

"It's doubtful whether God can bless a man greatly until He has hurt him deeply," said A. W. Tozer. In weakness, God's strength can be revealed. Joseph was jailed, David driven into hiding, Paul imprisoned, and Christ crucified, but even in defeat, God's servants are not destroyed.

Part of the miracle of grace is that broken vessels can be made whole, with even more capacity than before.

7

The Best Defense

You must live with people to know their problems, and live with God in order to solve them.

P. T. Forsyth

With the right spirit, a clumsy church structure will work. Without the right spirit, an ideal structure won't work.

Malcolm Cronk

After looking at the diverse dragons that can threaten a church, what are the best defenses?

Landscapers know the best way to prevent weeds is not to attack them individually. Uprooting stubborn dandelions or chickweeds one by one will improve appearances temporarily, but within days, the troublesome plants will be back.

The best way to handle weeds is a thick, healthy lawn, which keeps them from springing up in the first place.

Likewise pastors, who are charged to "see to it . . . that no bitter root grows up to cause trouble and defile many" (Hebrews 12:15), find that the best way to prevent dragon blight, or at least minimize its damage, is to concentrate on developing a healthy church.

Taking opportunities to build a close, cohesive church will produce better results than the shrewdest political maneuvers to squelch dissenters after problems sprout. Defusing potential problems before they arise is far better than troubleshooting later on.

What are the keys to dragon-proofing a church? Obviously no technique is 100-percent effective, but there are several principles pastors have found helpful in building church health.

Encourage a Positive Atmosphere

Some churches enjoy fighting. So do some pastors. Feisty, do-or-die leaders have a way of developing feisty churches.

Joseph Bayly, a savvy observer of church life, once wrote: "Fighters must fight. Generals and admirals are never so happy as when they are involved in a big or little war. Boxers are never so happy as when they are pounding opponents insensate. Battling pastors and battling churches are never so happy as when they are locked in combat, preferably with enemies without, but otherwise with each other."

When attacked by church members, some pastors react by retaliating or at least refusing on principle to compromise.

To bend would be a sign of weakness. It's total victory, unconditional surrender—or perish gloriously in the attempt. Peacemaking, to them, is seen as compromise.

When relationships become adversarial, however, the pastor's days are numbered. Most congregations are capable of producing more dragons than any one pastor can deal with. The best defense is to create an atmosphere that breeds mutual advocates, not adversaries.

How? Not by refusing to fight, necessarily—some important battles may have to be waged, although less frequently than most of us think. More often, the best way to build an atmosphere of cooperation is to model a positive tone personally:

- by praising publicly the congregation's strengths
- by enjoying and taking pride in the diversity among church members
- by thanking critics, at least initially, for their candor and concern
- by assuming anything uncomplimentary you say about anyone will be repeated—because it probably will be—and by trusting very few people (your spouse? a colleague?) with your private criticisms and suspicions
- by being slow to step into other people's disagreements—balancing Paul's instruction to carry, with some qualifications, each other's burdens (Galatians 6:1–5) and Jesus' refusal to intervene in the disputes of others (Luke 12:14).

One pastor who has seen his nondenominational church transformed from a defeated, divided group to an enthusiastic, high-morale congregation says, "Obviously the Holy

Spirit is responsible for this kind of change, but I think he honored some of our efforts in that direction, too. We began focusing on the joys of life rather than bemoaning our discouragements. You don't cover up your disappointments, failed programs, and lost votes, but neither do you dwell on them or announce them from the pulpit."

Pastors who personify a nondefensive spirit of joy and generosity tend not to attract as many dragons. And when they are attacked, the majority of the congregation begins to notice something amiss—"That's not the way we do things around here."

When the fruit of the Spirit becomes characteristic of the church's daily life, it becomes painfully clear whenever one person violates that spirit, and the body itself will work to take care of the irritation.

Get People Working in Ministry

Unemployment will breed discontentment, whether in Pennsylvania steel towns, inner cities, or the church. Those fully employed in significant ministry are less likely to become troublesome.

When Richard Halverson was pastor of First Presbyterian Church in Hollywood, California, a church of seven thousand members, he discovered to his amazement only 365 people were required to fill the church slots—choirs, boards, committees, teaching posts. And that was assuming each person could hold only one position. This meant, of course, that the overwhelming majority of the church could never have a personal ministry within the institution. As he observed in his book *How I Changed My Thinking About the Church*, "If the work of the church is what is done inside the institution, very few, relatively speaking, will ever have an opportunity to do the work of the church."

Smaller churches may have a higher percentage of people involved in maintaining the church program, but they still can't give everyone a job, nor should they. Some of the most significant ministry is not done inside the walls of the church but outside, where the gospel has its most visible effect.

Elton Trueblood says one of the worst true stories he knows is about the preacher who stood on Laymen's Sunday, the first Sunday in October, and preached on lay ministry. He was so stirring and persuasive that at the end, when he said, "Will those who are willing to dedicate themselves to the lay ministry please come forward?" a hundred people responded. Someone standing close to the pastor heard him mutter, "Oh my, what am I going to do with a hundred ushers?" The pastor had missed the point of his own sermon.

When it comes to breeding dragons, underemployment can be just as bad as unemployment. Maybe worse. Petty jobs lead to petty conflicts. But problems seldom arise from those active in significant people ministries. Attacks are rare from those concerned with ministering to others—whether in a Bible class, or children's club program, or outside the church among refugees, the homeless, co-workers, a neighborhood Bible study, international students, the elderly, a support group, tutoring, or in any other situation of applying the gospel to people's needs week after week.

Like any army, those on the front lines don't have time to complain. Griping is the luxury of those with small jobs.

Being in the battle isn't always fun or even desirable to those involved, but it certainly has more significance and provides more motivation than bureaucratic work.

In the church, administrative details and paperwork are necessary. After all, someone must decide who's going to mow the church lawn, what color to paint the nursery, and who will serve on the kitchen committee. But a church overloaded with bureaucratic ministries is a prime target for a dragon attack.

A ministering laity, not just a busy laity, is a key to suppressing the dragon population.

Reinforce the Productive Members

A ministering laity doesn't happen naturally. Many people still expect the pastor to do the ministry while they watch—and criticize. Changing that image requires shaking up time priorities. Pastors who develop strong volunteer leaders have learned to honor those who minister, not those who demand it.

Church members notice whom the pastor chooses to spend time with. They appreciate pastors ministering to the chronic dependents, but they lose respect if the emotionally needy or the "squeaky wheels" get most of the pastor's attention. Worse, they begin to assume the pastor is the designated minister, and valuable opportunities for building active ministries by the members are lost. A breeding ground for dragons begins to develop. Even if the solid, ministering laypeople are not taken for granted, often they aren't given the time they deserve.

"One of the things that surprised me when I entered the pastorate was that people felt they had to have a problem to talk to me," says a Denver pastor. "All I heard was 'Pastor, I don't know what to do,' and the healthy, productive people never made appointments because they felt I was too busy."

This pastor has since let the church know he no longer does extended counseling. "I'm available to see anyone for counseling *once*," he says. "After that, I refer them to a professional or one of our trained lay counselors. This still keeps me available to everyone and keeps me in touch with individual hurts, but it's freed me to spend those hours with ministry-minded people strategizing how to minister in the workplace or launch a new ministry or do an old one better."

He's also discovered it helps in dragon prevention. The respected people in the congregation are not the self-appointed critics but the doers. Initiative is encouraged. Because of the pastor's time priorities, newcomers to the church soon learn that the church's attitude toward new lay ministries is: Better to have tried and failed than never to have tried at all.

Know the Congregational Values

Pastors, especially those in their first year with a church, need to take time to build trust and healthy relationships before initiating changes.

Church analyst and former pastor Roy Oswald observes that the task of the first twelve months is to be "a lover and a historian—to fully understand what has taken place here and to learn to love these people before making changes." Too many quick changes tells the people, "You don't understand Christianity. I'm the expert, you need to do it my way."

"I know one young woman who started pastoring in a small town," said Oswald in *Leadership Journal*, "and she thought it ridiculous that the pulpit Bible was a huge King James, which didn't leave room for her notes. So she put it away. The next week it appeared back on the pulpit with a note: 'This Bible belongs on the pulpit. (Signed) The Management.' She refused to give in and removed the Bible again. She began having major problems in that congregation, largely because she couldn't recognize what was valuable to those people."[1]

Pastors of healthy churches have learned what Dietrich Bonhoeffer called "honoring the Christ that is present in the community"—discovering what the Holy Spirit has been doing prior to their arrival. Even sick congregations have a spark of spiritual life that can be found and fanned into flame.

This kind of assessment isn't limited to new pastors. Veterans as well can back off projects for a time to repair relationships.

One Presbyterian pastor, who is used by his denomination to counsel beleaguered colleagues, observes that "time and again I see pastors feeling they have to come across forcefully to maintain their position of authority or else they'll be disregarded. But the opposite happens. They diminish their authority by pushing too hard. Real authority comes from proven credibility and caring."

Rick Richardson, who teaches leadership and evangelism at Wheaton College, writes: "In the past, being an expert and having the answers were what built credibility and a hearing. Today, having the same questions, struggles, and hurts is what builds credibility and gains a hearing." Knowing how to listen and to articulate the questions, struggles, and hurts is what strengthens leadership.

Not many situations are solved by force. Most churches have plenty of strong personalities but a shortage of gentleness. Often the pastor gains more influence by being a gentle friend than by grabbing for control.

Share Outside Interests

If pastors are all business with their congregations, they lose opportunities to build pressure release valves to use when dragons cause things to heat up.

A trustee and former custodian in a Kentucky church was making life miserable for the present janitor. He would leave notes for certain floors to be swept or lights to be turned off. He tried to impose a watering schedule for the church lawn. After a public confrontation with the janitor over a thermostat setting, the trustee was asked to come to the next elder board meeting.

"Fred, we know you've got an interest in the maintenance of the church building, but we hired another man to do the job," the board chairman said. "Our custodian reports to the pastor, and we think it's best if you stay out of the picture."

"I don't think the custodian is doing much of a job," Fred said. "And if you don't get him out of there, I don't see how I can continue in good conscience to serve as a trustee."

There was a long silence before the board chairman said, "We're not asking for your resignation, Fred. But we've hired a man to do a job. His supervisor is satisfied with his work.

And we can't fire him just because you don't like him." Fred stalked out of the meeting without the issue being resolved.

The pastor, however, shared a ride with Fred each week to their Monday night bowling league. Though he wasn't looking forward to the encounter, he knew someone had to help Fred settle things.

Nothing but bowling was discussed for two hours, but finally on the way home Fred said, "You know, Pastor, I guess I was out of line yesterday. I'll try to let things go and let the new guy do his job."

Later the pastor observed, "I was glad we both liked bowling. I don't know if Fred would have reacted so well if I had just barged into his home to talk things over."

Other pastors let their passion for softball, poetry, or country music be known. Far from isolating them, these interests make pastors more human, more accessible, which often helps in finding common ground with a dragon.

Even family needs can provide a foundation for friendship. One pastor found his children helped heal a deteriorating relationship with a board member. At the height of their disagreement over a building program, the board member developed a genuine fondness for the pastor's children.

"My wife was in the choir," the pastor says. "The kids needed to sit with someone in church, and they grew attached to Dick and Verla Martin. Before long, Dick and Verla were offering to baby-sit if we needed someone. We took them up on it."

Later Dick told the pastor, "I've changed my mind on the building program. It was your girls who won me over. I was suspicious of your motives, but now that I know your girls, I feel like I know you and I trust you."

The pastor observes, "I was so glad we'd been careful not to let the kids pick up our bad vibrations with the Martins. We want our girls to grow up loving the church, not turned off because of hostilities among members. If they'd been defensive, I don't think God could have used them to heal our relationship with Dick and Verla."

Even the love for children and the need for a baby-sitter can be used to defuse tension.

Underselling Beats Overselling

There's a temptation, especially in smaller churches, to be so eager for growth that you tell prospective members whatever they want to hear. After all, if you've got only ten families, you're desperate for more, and you unwittingly present the church as a perfect fit for their needs.

Overselling the church, pastors have found, is a mistake. While it's flattering to have new members, they're likely to become dragons and eventually do the church more harm than good if they come with an ideology that doesn't mesh with the church's DNA. A small, cohesive family is better than a house divided, even a large house.

"I've changed my approach after several bad experiences," says a Baptist church planter. "I no longer say, 'Our church is for everyone.' I'm more realistic now. Everyone is welcome, but I make it clear our church has a particular personality that will appeal to some and not others. Now I say, 'This is the direction we're going. If you're going the same direction, we'd love to have you hop on.'"

Those who prefer formal liturgy ought not to be persuaded to join a church that majors in the extemporaneous. Charismatics and noncharismatics can belong to the same congregation, but they need to know the ground rules before they join.

"I enjoy my charismatic friends, but our church is not charismatic," says the pastor of a Bible church in Oklahoma. "They're welcome in our church, but I make clear from the beginning that we worship in a different way, and if they're uncomfortable with our style, they should probably find another church in town."

With a grin he tells about one woman who'd visited the church several times before eventually joining a charismatic church down the street. When the Bible church pastor visited the woman, he asked, "What attracts you to the other church?"

"It's so friendly—they always hug me there," she said.

"Well, we hug a bit, too," the pastor said.

"Yeah, but they *really* hug."

After that conversation, the pastor realized the issue was as much one of style and expression as it was about theology.

"Our church is friendly. Five different people from our church had been over to see her, and no one from the other church had called on her," the pastor reflects. "But they *hugged* her. And that's what means the most to her. That style doesn't come naturally for most of our people. So the right thing was to encourage her to join the other church."

Prospects have a right to know what a church is and isn't. Presenting a fuzzy picture of the church's stand and style is a sure way to produce confusion and dissension.

Healthy churches are confident in their own identity. They know their direction and limits. And they're less likely to be tossed about by disillusioned dragons.

8

The Second-Best Defense

He that cannot obey, cannot command.

Benjamin Franklin

If the church itself is not healthy, the best thing to do is to build a healthy board. Cohesiveness among the spiritual leaders of the congregation is a healthy core for healing the rest of the body and for fighting the infectious attitudes that spring up from time to time.

Some pastors go too far and "stack" the board with friends who can be trusted never to disagree.

"Every member of my board is someone I've personally led to Christ, and I've never had trouble with them," boasted one prominent Southern pastor to a group of seminarians. "I held one man in my arms as he went through delirium tremens. Now he's on my board, and I can count on his vote. He *owes* me."

Such crass political maneuvering is not only repugnant but, in the long run, runs against the pastor's best interest. The best board is not one where everyone plays follow-the-leader. A board that always votes unanimously the pastor's way will only be as strong as the pastor's personality. When the pastor is overwhelmed, run down, and needing guidance, a collection of clones won't be adequate.

The most effective boards can see issues from different sides and examine them fully, even when it means disagreeing with the pastor.

At the same time, healthy boards are united in purpose and plan, respecting one another's differences. The strongest board is a team of co-workers willing to honor God not only with their decisions but also with the decision-making process. Their relationships are as important as their righteousness, and the relationship between pastor and board is cemented with trust; without that, the pastor's ministry will inevitably come unglued.

Cultivating Personal Trust

No pastor would consciously take the relationship with the board for granted, but one pastor, Mack Sawyer, made the mistake of thinking that a trust relationship with three or four individual board members was good enough. It wasn't.

For several years, Mack had sensed some resistance from a couple of elders but didn't think it serious. Don Albert, a member of the executive committee, seemed particularly distant. Each year he would question Mack's proposed budget and second-guess his equipment expenditures. But since Mack had a good relationship with the church chairman and most of the other board members, he didn't worry too much about Don. *That's just Don,* he figured, *a tightwad.*

After six years at the church, Mack was invited to candidate as a minister of discipleship at a large church in California. He'd been thinking about his future, wondering what God wanted him to do for the rest of his life, and while he was happy pastoring a smaller church, he was willing to be led elsewhere.

Wanting to be up-front but discreet, Mack told the executive committee where he would be that weekend. The visit to California, however, only confirmed his desire to continue pastoring a smaller church.

But unknown to Mack, it made Don even more suspicious.

Matters suddenly came to a head six months later when Mack was invited to speak at Spiritual Emphasis Week at his denomination's college. His job description allowed three weekends a year for outside speaking. For a whole week at once, however, Mack thought he should mention it to the executive committee, though he expected their support and blessing.

As the five—church chairman Harry Anderson, Don Albert, Mack, and two other board members—sat in the pastor's office, they chatted pleasantly for several minutes, took care of several agenda items, and then Mack told them about his opportunity to speak at the college. He was totally unprepared for the reaction.

Don Albert immediately challenged the request. "I don't think the pastor should leave for a week when the ministry here is in a shambles. Why should we let you go elsewhere when there are such terrible deficiencies here?"

Mack didn't want to defend his ministry, though he could have pointed to a stable to slightly rising attendance, several new volunteers working with the church youth, and four or five home Bible studies, including one in Don's home. After all, these men knew the situation as well as he did.

Mack looked at the other board members, who remained silent. Was this "just Don"? Or was there something Mack was missing?

Mack tried to joke. "Well, if there are deficiencies, I doubt if five days without me would move them to the crisis stage. My being away just might be what the church needs." Then, turning to the church chairman, Mack asked, "Harry, what do you think?"

"Excuse me, you all," Harry said. "It's late, and I've got to pick up my daughter from her gymnastics class. I'm sure you four can work this out." Mack sagged as his closest friend on the board walked out.

Finally one of the other board members spoke. "Mack, where do you see your career going in the days ahead?"

"I honestly don't know," Mack said. "I'm happy here, but you all know I'd like to get my D.Min. someday."

"Maybe it would be better to use your outside speaking time to start working on your degree."

It was a reasonable idea, but a bit off the subject, Mack thought. He began to realize maybe the committee members saw him as disloyal for candidating at another church. Perhaps they saw this request to speak elsewhere as an indication he was still looking around for greener pasture, though he honestly wasn't.

"The question was not whether I would represent the church well at the college or whether I would be able to minister there," Mack says in retrospect. "It wasn't even a question of having the bases covered back at the church. They were. To this day, I don't know what the real question was."

Looking back on the rest of that meeting, Mack recalls, "I don't remember the rest of what happened, but I walked out of there a crushed person. The entire validity of my ministry had been called into question, and no one said a word in my defense. My best friend had walked out, unwilling to take a stand. I went home and cried. I asked God, *Am I of any value in this church? Does everyone feel like Don Albert?* These were my church leaders, the ones I reported to. What were they trying to tell me?

"At that point, I knew I was leaving the church. It was only a question of when."

Nine months later, Mack resigned to accept a teaching position in a Christian high school.

What was Mack's mistake? "I'd built a marvelous relationship with a few board members but not all. I'd never even had coffee with Don Albert. We'd never had a warm conversation about his family, his goals in life, or his dreams for the church. I knew him only as an irascible tightwad to be avoided or worked around. I knew we didn't get along, but I figured you can't be close to everyone. In the end, he held the balance for my credibility in ministry and my viability as pastor in that congregation."

If pastors and their boards don't trust each other, the church will be unhealthy, and chances are, the pastor's tenure will be brief and unpleasant. Some boards don't allow a pastor to win their trust; they see it as their job to "keep the pastor in line." Unless the relationship changes, that ministry is doomed. A relationship of trust must be built, even when it doesn't come naturally.

Sometimes this relationship takes time—several years, perhaps—as certain members move off the board and new blood takes their place. Always, however, the responsibility for trying to develop trust lies with the pastor.

"The best thing we've done," says a Mennonite pastor in Pennsylvania, "is to set aside four evenings a year where the seven elders and I have dinner together, spend an hour with each person sharing what's happening in his life, pray for personal needs, and then talk about the ministry—not specific business items, but our vision for the church, our goals. We've dreamed what our congregation can become, and that's helped put things in perspective and built our respect for one another.

"It's helped build the feeling among us that when disagreements come, we know we can at least trust one another's intentions."

Many pastors have mentioned that a breakthrough came when they began revealing some of their spiritual struggles and their fears for the church. Often board members won't open up until the pastor gives permission by letting his own humanness and vulnerability show.

Sometimes experienced pastors and lay leaders from other churches can help that process begin.

One young pastor of a struggling rural church was in perpetual conflict with the board until he invited a pastor and key layman from another church in the district to guide the annual leadership retreat. Among other questions, the visitors asked, "What fears do you have for this church?" Slowly, what everyone had been thinking but never articulated before began to come out: "I guess I'm not sure our church will be able to survive another ten years of dwindling population in our community. The economy around here means that very few younger adults are able to find employment."

As the young pastor and board were able to admit the uncertainties of the future and the possibility that the church might have to close its doors eventually, they began to better understand one another. Their strained relationship began to heal.

Personal relationships, mutual respect, and trust are the foundation of a strong working relationship between pastor and board. But there are other important elements to keep dragons from emerging within the board. Churches that emphasize these elements not only develop strong, ministering boards but find attacks by outside dragons are easier to handle.

Chosen for Character, Not Clout

To paraphrase Peter DeVries, we're attracted to individuals because of a personality, but after that we have to live with a character. Healthy boards are built with members selected for their spiritual qualifications—wisdom, resilience, faith, and love—not just because they have money, longevity in the congregation, or strong personalities.

Thousands of congregations have horror stories about the "good ol' boy" approach to selecting church leaders: Someone is well liked and willing to serve and thus is considered qualified, but within a few years, the church regrets the decision because of the elder's (choose any of the following) adultery, arrest, divorce, shady business practices, or domineering and manipulative style.

First Timothy 3 and Titus 1 list the spiritual qualities to look for in potential church leaders—such things as being temperate, controlled, hospitable, and free from greed—which is certainly a better list than well liked, willing to serve, and able to tithe $25,000 a year.

Even with this list of spiritual qualities, though, how do you gauge spiritual maturity? How can you venture opinions of someone's qualifications without becoming judgmental? While no objective criteria are specified in Scripture, several of the qualities do suggest a basis for selecting elders and deacons.

They must have proven their ability to minister and to give spiritual encouragement. They must have a spirit of hospitality, which means people feel welcome in their presence. They must be "apt to teach," that is, able to explain the faith and help others grow. They must have a reputation in their community and among their co-workers as being consistently Christian. And they must not be new believers—they must be known well enough and long enough to have been observed living out their faith.

"It takes time to see someone demonstrating Christian maturity, wisdom, and compassion," says an Assembly of God pastor. "So our congregation has a rule that a person has to be a member for at least a year before being considered for office. And because we don't hurry people into membership, most of our new members have been in the fellowship two or three years. That means candidates for the board have all served in other areas of the church's life and have demonstrated their gifts, abilities, and commitment."

A Board, Not Individual Planks

Sometimes new members of the governing board of the church don't understand their role. They assume that becoming an elder means having spiritual authority as an individual, and the responsibility to exercise their authority as an individual. This misunderstanding quickly leads to problems.

"One of our new elders almost underwent a personality change," said the chairman of the board at a nondenominational church in the Midwest. "Before he became an elder, he was an encourager and a very positive person. But upon becoming an elder, he started sitting in on youth group meetings and telling the youth leaders what they needed to be doing. Almost every week, he was giving the worship leaders a critique of the service."

When the chairman heard about this from the youth and worship leaders, he asked the new elder about the feedback he was giving these ministry leaders.

"I was elected to be an elder, responsible to oversee the ministry of the church," the man said. "I take my job seriously, and if I'm going to be responsible for the health of the church, I don't know how else to do the job other than to monitor and give constructive input."

Immediately the chairman recognized the problem.

The new elder assumed that being an elder was something to be done as an individual. In actuality, it was a group responsibility.

"I explained that the role of the elder board is to speak as one, not to be speaking as individual elders. Our authority rests in what the group decides, not what individuals think.

"Individually, we are to be active and involved and supportive church members, but we have no special authority as individuals just because we are serving on the elder board. Our authority comes when we consider issues as a group and come to a group decision as it pertains to church governance."

The new elder hadn't understood that distinction.

"That actually takes a load off my shoulders," he told the chairman. "I want to do a good job as an elder, and I assumed that meant doing so as an individual. Being part of the governance team takes the pressure off."

Now the church makes sure to brief new elders on the corporate role of the elder board.

Common Learning Experiences

"Each month our deacons read a book on church renewal, church government, or some other aspect of church life," says a suburban Minneapolis pastor. At each month's board meeting, at least half an hour is spent discussing the concepts in the book. The ideas also become the basis of informal conversations over coffee or lunch.

Periodically, a major portion of the board meeting is spent discussing a case study or a written assignment one of the deacons has completed. At least once a year, each deacon attends a seminar, a conference, or a webinar with another deacon and they report back to the board.

This exposure to leadership principles and what other churches are doing has broadened the board's perspective and made for healthier and more well-informed discussions.

"For the first time, those who had been the biggest pains in the church understand where we're going. We're using the same vocabulary, and we have a common base of understanding," says the pastor.

That's not stacking the board; that's strengthening it.

Regular Performance Reviews

"If my board isn't happy with my performance, I don't want to be the second one to know about it," says a Bible church pastor. "If they aren't behind me, I'll leave. I wouldn't want to be in a church where the recognized spiritual leadership cannot support my ministry. But with their support, I'm free to minister without feeling threatened by the criticisms of others."

Evaluations, preferably written, not only help pastors synchronize their ministries with the priorities of the board, but also become an excellent defense when the pastor is criticized. Critics can be told, "I'm doing what I've been commissioned to do," and complaints can be referred to the board.

Reviews also help prevent surprise attacks by individual board members, and even if they occur, the evaluation provides a forum for those criticisms to be fully discussed and defused.

Accepting the Defense Contract

Members of healthy boards understand that sometimes their job includes defense.

They are decision-making diplomats. They may debate issues, but when decisions are made, they become ambassadors to defend those decisions even if they didn't vote for them. Many pastors let their board members know from the beginning that though they may differ sharply in their meetings, in public they do not dissent but represent the will of the board.

Defending the ministry also means defending the church from attack. Some pastors brief new board members that part of their task is to help shepherd the flock, and sometimes that means protection. If ministry calls for a private confrontation, and the pastor feels he shouldn't go alone, elders should be willing to go along. If there are emergencies, elders should know they may be called in the middle of the night.

The clear guidance and support of elders keep a pastor effective, and pastors minister most effectively when they are not defensive. At times, the board can deflect criticism aimed at the pastor and confront the church dragons. Occasionally this means taking a gossiping member aside and saying, "We don't belittle our pastor in this church; if he's doing something wrong, please come to us before spreading this kind of talk." Other times it means facing critics openly.

When an Evangelical Free church in Washington decided to add a bell tower to its building, several members voiced strong opposition in the business meeting. After the vote, 94–8 in favor of the construction, the elders invited one member, the loudest dissenter, to their next meeting. They wanted to prevent any continuing guerrilla warfare.

After saying, "We want to be sensitive to the points you made in the congregational meeting," and listening to his current feelings about the bell tower, the board chairman said, "We want you to know we respect your position. It does have merit, but we've decided to go another direction. We want you to know how we arrived at our decision, and we'd like you to try to see the full picture." After going through the reasons for the bell tower, he said, "Now we want to know if you'll be able to support the decision of the church." They asked what he would be saying to others about the issue.

"The spirit of the meeting defused his anger," says the pastor. "He felt as though he'd been heard. It prevented his going to other people in the congregation and mouthing off, which could have done a lot of harm."

The board has done this on three or four potentially volatile issues in the last two years. "It helps people to know the board is willing to listen even though they disagree," says the pastor. "Often the elder board is seen as a powerful group that sits behind a table and makes big decisions regardless of what anyone says. We've tried to break that down and let people see that our board members love the Lord, they love people, and they love this ministry."

A side benefit has been that by kindly confronting dissenters, the board has not only prevented serious dragons but has become more unified in the process.

Meetings a Ministry, Not a Misery

The atmosphere of the board meeting itself is an excellent gauge of the church's health. Do board members pray for one another? Do they take time to find out one another's worries and joys? Time spent in personal ministry at the beginning of a board meeting is time well spent. An unwritten agenda item at every healthy board meeting is "Encouraging each other."

One Baptist pastor, however, discovered this didn't happen in his board meetings until he changed the time and place. Meeting on Sunday afternoons in a church classroom seemed to produce sparks. He always found himself pressured, feeling backed into a corner.

In the process of building a new wing, one Sunday afternoon the deacon board reviewed the plans of six architects, and each of the six board members supported a different architect's plans. The temperature of the discussion rose, and the pastor found himself in the middle, trying to keep peace, and sensing hostility all around. Finally he'd had enough.

"Let's cool it," he said testily. "I don't want to talk anymore about this. We don't seem to be making progress, and I've got to go preach in the evening service in less than an hour." And he dismissed the meeting.

A short while later, stomach still churning, "I had to go talk about the sweet love of Jesus, and the board members all went home and watched TV. They didn't even come to the evening service," the pastor remembers.

The next day, the pastor wrote an email to all boards, committees, and councils: "Sometimes we're in danger of developing Christians who are all legs and no heart. And I don't want to be guilty of that by overloading the schedule on Sunday, which should be set aside for worship and rest. From now on, there will be no more Sunday afternoon business meetings."

"The deacons had been the key infringers," says the pastor. "I didn't know—maybe they'd blast me for making this decision unilaterally—but sometimes you can do something like this through the War Powers Act and get away with it."

Instead of blasting him, the deacons blessed him, with three of them replying, "This is a good decision. We wanted to be home with our families anyway, not spending all day running to church. Thanks."

Now the deacons meet in the pastor's family room on Monday night, and while it wouldn't be accurate to say that arguments have disappeared and the pastor's stomach never churns, it is true that the climate is improved. As the pastor says, "It's harder to be angry with someone after you've prayed for him, when you're sitting on the same couch, and you have a glass of iced tea in your hand."

Developing a healthy board doesn't guarantee a healthy church, nor does a healthy church guarantee a dragon-free existence, but certainly the healthier the church the less damage dragons can inflict.

When dragons do emerge, even in healthy churches with healthy boards, some specific skills are needed. Sometimes dragons will have legitimate criticisms, and they need to be recognized, addressed, and applauded. Other times, when the dragons are on a rampage, they will need to be confronted. And still other times, churches must simply learn to cope with unresolved situations.

9

When the Dragon May Be Right

Get a friend to tell you your faults, or better still, welcome
an enemy who will watch you keenly and sting you savagely.
What a blessing such an irritating critic will be to a wise man,
what an intolerable nuisance to a fool!

Charles Spurgeon

Nobody enjoys criticism, especially from dragons. Their
"constructive" observations often come across like a wreck-
ing ball—maybe beneficial in the long run, but the immediate
effect is noise, rubble, and a large hole in your motivation.

Yet even dragons can sometimes be right, and almost all
pastors are willing to benefit if the criticism is valid. As Proverbs 17:10 says, "A rebuke impresses a discerning person more
than a hundred lashes a fool."

The problem is deciding which criticisms are valid and which are unjustified. It requires a tough hide and a sensitive heart. And a few specific criteria don't hurt. Here are several tests pastors have identified to help distinguish fair from unfair attacks.

Consider the source. The first test is the motivation of the critics. Are they truly well-intentioned? Are they committed to ministry? Do they want the best for the church? Are they people of integrity? Are they self-aware enough to understand the issue and accept their share of the responsibility or blame?

Psalm 141:5 says, "Let a righteous man strike me—that is a kindness; let him rebuke me—that is oil on my head. My head will not refuse it." The righteous, those of integrity who are spiritually mature, must be taken more seriously than impulsive dragons.

The number of sources making the same criticism is also telling. Church dragons often claim, "It isn't just me; a lot of other people feel this way." But the "lot of other people" is usually a very small faction. Unless those other people step forward, you can afford to be skeptical. Pastors can apply 1 Timothy 5:19 even when the charges are laid against themselves—"Do not entertain an accusation against an elder unless it is brought by two or three witnesses."

Solitary shots should be ignored, but when they come from several directions, it's time to pay attention. As someone once said, "If one calls you a donkey, ignore him. If two call you a donkey, check for hoofprints. If three call you a donkey, get a saddle."

Consider the spirit in which the criticism is given. Gauge the emotional climate. Does this particular criticism come out of rational reflection or emotional fervor? From weeks of observation or hours of upset? Fair criticism, like fertilizer, should be gentle enough to nourish a person's growth without destroying the roots.

Sometimes criticism is the only way a person knows how to initiate conversation. It's a way of getting attention before moving into the real subject he wants to discuss.

If a person takes the time to talk privately, in person, however, and assures you of his love and loyalty before offering his criticism, and is willing to help with the solution, it's more likely to be a fair criticism. At least he's thought it through and is committed to solving the problem.

James D. Glasse described the distinction this way: "I would rather be disagreed with by someone who understands me than to be agreed with by someone who does not understand me."

Unfair criticisms are more likely to be received over the phone, in passing at the rear of the sanctuary after the service, in a caustic email, or indirectly via a third party who tells you, "Mrs. Canfield is upset with the new songs we're singing."

Another factor is determining whether the person really wants to help or just likes to carp. A deacon in an Indiana church is in the habit of calling the pastor each Sunday afternoon and "evaluating" the morning service. "I told him that Sunday afternoons were a bad time for me," says the pastor, "that I was drained from preaching, and it wasn't the best time to be getting feedback. If he really wanted to help, he should see me during the week." The Sunday afternoon calls continued.

"I don't take those kinds of criticisms seriously," says the pastor. "Now I let his calls go to voice mail, or else I read the paper while he drones on over the phone."

Consider hot anger a sign that something more is involved. Sometimes a dragon is so angry you're almost paralyzed by the outburst. "If I had attacked his wife in front of the congregation, I could expect such anger," says a pastor who's still puzzled. "But all I said was . . ."

The natural reaction is to try to pacify the irate accuser at all costs. Silence, however, is usually the best defense.

If the anger is out of proportion to the issues raised, chances are the real issue hasn't surfaced. The only thing to do is hear out the person completely. Sometimes the catharsis will uncover the real problem.

"It was one of those rare professional moments," says an Episcopal rector in Ohio. "I didn't react nor did I get angry. I just listened as he went on for twenty minutes. His voice was loud and strident. His list of grievances seemed endless: This was wrong with the Christian education program; that was wrong with maintenance. I was at the center of it all.

"Suddenly, almost in mid-sentence, he blurted out, 'She says all I'm interested in is sex.' For the next hour we talked about his marriage difficulties. The 'issues' were never raised again."

If the underlying issues don't emerge, it's time to use trusted elders or other laypeople to help the dragon sort through the feelings. You may have to coach them on how to approach the dragon. For instance, one tactic the mediator might try: "Hank, we've been friends a long time. I care about you, and I'm sorry you're so angry. Everyone knows our pastor isn't perfect; yet your anger seems out of proportion to the situation. Is there more to it than what I've heard?"

Problems at work, personal pain, financial setbacks, or grief over a recent loss may produce unresolved anger the dragon doesn't know how to deal with, emotions he may not even admit to himself. So he unloads on the minister because ministers don't usually fight back. Helping the dragon realize there's more than the surface issue will offer the opportunity for growth.

Another approach is saying to the angry person, "Let's look at this issue for a minute and see what the likely consequences are. What's the worst possible thing the pastor's position could lead to? Would the rest of the church allow that to happen?" Calmly putting into words the probable chain of events sometimes makes the dragon realize eternity isn't at stake.

If the criticism passes the source and spirit tests, then *consider it prayerfully.* In 2 Kings 19, Hezekiah offers a good model. When Jerusalem was besieged by the Assyrian hordes, Sennacherib, a not-so-well-intentioned dragon, sent a taunting, critical letter to the king of Judah. Hezekiah took it from the messenger, read it, went up to the temple, "and spread it out before the Lord" (v. 14).

In dealing with a dragon's criticisms, we too can spread them out before the Lord, asking him to show us what is true in them. If something there is valid, the Lord will help us benefit from it. If it's all unjustified, we can say, "The insults that have fallen on me, Lord, have fallen on you too" (see Psalm 69:9).

Consider concrete criticisms more seriously. Complaints that are vague and general, such as "I'm not being fed" or "I'm not growing," usually say more about the complainers than the church. They may actually be overfed but under-exercised. Those genuinely needing less milk and more meat will probably be able to be more specific in their requests and offer their own helpful ideas.

Likewise, if people criticize things you can't change (your age, for instance) or things they knew and accepted when they called you (your preaching style), the criticisms are probably unfair.

"Some people demand 'evangelistic messages,' but what they really mean is they want an evangelistic invitation after every sermon," says a South Dakota pastor. Others want to hear certain familiar words in each sermon or expect a certain style.

On the other hand, take specific criticism of sermons seriously. If people complain about theological language, big words, or length of sermons, it's obvious your sermons are not communicating, and putting God's Word in language people can understand is the purpose of a sermon.

One preacher was criticized for his grammar by a former English teacher. After her third complaint, instead of reacting defensively, the pastor admitted his schooling had been weak in that area and asked her where he could sign up for a night class. He took a quarter of adult education at a community college, and despite his subsequent occasional lapses of grammar, the former teacher became one of his strongest supporters.

Consider the criticism calmly. A veteran pastor in Toronto has a standard reply to every criticism: "You may be right."

"By saying that, I haven't conceded a thing," he explains. "It gives me time to mull it over, it tells the critic I'm taking the observation seriously, but it doesn't commit me to a particular response."

Other pastors respond, "Let's talk about that this week. Will you give me a call to set up a time to talk?" which leaves the initiative with the critic and tests how strongly the complaint is felt.

Since most pastors get the bulk of criticism on Sunday, when they're weary and emotionally spent, this delaying action is especially helpful.

"Never deal with criticism on the same day it's received," says the Toronto pastor, "especially on Sunday. In fact, I usually can't deal with it until Tuesday. Psychologically and physically, I'm used up; too much adrenaline has been pumped."

Consider criticisms corporately. Objective friends, a spouse, or private conversations with individual board members can provide perspective.

Sometimes we can read into comments criticisms that weren't intended. "One person told me, 'You spend a lot of time telling stories in your sermons,'" says a Colorado minister. "I didn't have time to ask him to elaborate, but I thought he meant I was simplistic. Later the man's small group leader reported the man had told him he'd finally found a church where he could understand the sermon. What I'd taken as a criticism was actually a compliment."

More serious criticisms should be weighed by the church board as a whole. Referring a dragon to the board, where the issue can be discussed and decided corporately, is not just passing the buck. It's enlisting help in evaluating the validity of recurring criticisms. And besides, they have to live with you and whatever response you decide to make.

Often certain individuals will go to a conference or hear a particular speaker, and they come back saying the church ought to fit this great idea into its ministry. They don't consider how it would affect the total church program or where it should fit in the list of priorities. Those questions must be decided by the board, those appointed to give direction to the church.

Finally, *complete your consideration.* Criticisms can't be left unresolved indefinitely. At least mentally, it is better to decide within several days whether this criticism is something to act on or something to forget. Fretting week after week is the worst response.

"I have a wonderful spiritual gift—the gift of amnesia," says an Illinois pastor. "When I came to this church, I asked the Lord for two things: the ability to remember names and biographies, and the ability to forget situations. I work at forgetting the things I've heard that I can't do anything about, and the Lord has honored my efforts. It's a wonderful, wonderful thing. It's not denial or a psychological trick; it's simply processing criticisms and setting aside those I'm not able to respond to."

Many critics are only part-time dragons. They battle only infrequently. They may be hurt, ill, emotionally tied to a particular issue, or otherwise temporarily out of sync. The gift of amnesia is most helpful with these.

"The key to a discipling and reconciling ministry is to see that people change," says the Illinois pastor. "You must not dwell on what they were but what they are becoming and what they *can* become. The pastors I know who've gotten into the biggest trouble are those who can't let go of past hurts. They turn part-time dragons into full-time monsters."

Criticisms can't be ignored, nor should they be allowed to set the direction for the church. Every pastor walks that delicate line between steering and being steered by the congregation. As they weigh the criticisms, most ministers occasionally wonder, *Am I being followed or chased?*

Leadership Journal ran a one-liner that all too often describes the pastor's situation: "There go my people. I must hurry. I am their leader." This tension isn't all bad. A leader who takes no cues from the people is a dictator; the leader who tries to satisfy every critic is a "people pleaser" who gains neither respect nor effectiveness. Both extremes sabotage pastoral ministry. The pastor is not a dictator, arrogantly above criticism, nor is the pastor a garbage dump, passively accepting the abuse of the disgruntled.

"I've always felt the pastor's biblical authority is so high it's scary," says a seasoned Iowa minister. "But the pastoral office can only function in grace as it is honored and recognized by the people."

As such, the pastor leads more like a president than a dictator—leading, but only with the consent of the governed.

A pastor's authority requires two ingredients: God's appointment and call, and the body's respect for his leadership. Losing either side of the equation spells an end to effective ministry. Sensitivity to valid criticism and the ability to shrug off unfair comments will not help if the divine appointment is missing, but they can go a long way in producing the necessary respect within the body.

10

When It's Time to Confront

Every time we say, "I believe in the Holy Spirit," we mean
that we believe there is a living God able and willing to enter
human personality and change it.

J. B. Phillips

The intertestamental book Bel and the Dragon describes a
confrontation between Daniel and a great living dragon the
Babylonians revered. When Daniel was pressured to bow
before the monster, he said to the king, "If you will give me
permission, I will slay the dragon without sword or club."
The king agreed.

As verse 27 relates, "Then Daniel took pitch, fat, and hair,
and boiled them together and made cakes, which he fed to
the dragon. The dragon ate them, and burst open."

That's one kind of effective confrontation. Unfortunately, it's an approach that probably should not be used with dragons in the church. Unlike Daniel or Saint George, the goal of a pastor is not to slay but to tame the beast, to prevent further destruction on either side.

What Dragon Taming Is Not

Such work is rarely easy, never fun, but it is possible. Before looking at the important elements of effective confrontation, we must clarify what dragon taming is *not*.

Dragon taming is not suppressing differences of opinion. These are inevitable and even desirable—one person's insights balance another's quirks. The church is stronger when its unity comes out of diversity, when the body of Christ is more than birds of a feather flocking together. Unless the differing opinions are outright heresy or vitriol, they need not be feared.

Controlled friction produces energy, and energy is essential for creativity and effectiveness in church life. Different ideas should be allowed to coexist, and God allowed to take the lead, thereby raising one opinion to prominence.

A person is not a dragon because of different ideas but because of destructive actions.

Dragon taming is not silencing all complainers. Chronic complainers need to be deflected, not destroyed. Most gripers are low-octane hostiles who merely like to share their misery. Generally they're not destructive unless they're given the spotlight or made into martyrs. While their complaints aren't pleasant to hear, remember that complainers are rarely leaders themselves; their gripes are usually a symptom of their sense of powerlessness.

How do you handle complainers? Not by arguing—they're rarely willing to be convinced—but by letting them know there are other ways of looking at the situation. "You think Mark's presentation was rotten? That's interesting. I enjoy that kind of approach now and then."

Dragon taming is not giving in, becoming a doormat. Appeasing dragons and hoping they won't spew their wrath throughout the church rarely works long term. Simply because leaders are servants doesn't mean they must passively accept injustice or ignore threats to the body. Just a few sentences after writing those lofty verses on imitating Christ's humility and servanthood in Philippians 2, Paul warns, "Watch out for those dogs, those evildoers, those mutilators of the flesh" (3:2). Hardly all-welcoming words, but they're the words of a humble servant dedicated to protecting his Father's house.

What then is dragon taming? What is the point of any confrontation? Not stifling people's ideas but protecting the church from those *acting* in destructive ways. In that effort, the right attitude, atmosphere, and approach are essential.

The Attitude in Confronting

Often the greatest damage is not done by the dragons themselves but by the overreactions they provoke in others. When attacked by dragons, our normal response is to become upset or defensive, and when we feel threatened, we usually wind up trying to douse the fire by throwing gasoline on it.

In most disputes neither side is entirely innocent. And even if our cause is completely right, if we respond wrongly, we lose! The situation only gets worse.

The confrontation with dragons has to be carried out in love—smart love. "Always view the other person as a child of God like yourself," said one Arizona pastor. That is, of course, easier said than done.

The trick is to accept the dragon as a person of worth while not approving of his or her controlling tactics. It means trying to maintain an open relationship and keeping it current. Knowing what's going on in the lives of difficult members often proves helpful in their taming. Smart love also means trying to see the church and its perceived problems from their viewpoint.

One pastor resisted his impulse to ignore a young man who openly criticized him for moving too slowly to establish a small-group ministry. Instead, he spent time with the young man and discovered his doctors had recently found malignant cells in his blood. Suddenly he understood the young man's impatience and desire for community.

Pastors have discovered several helpful keys in establishing the right kind of attitude for dragon confrontation.

First, as early in the conflict as possible, someone must verbalize what Norm Shawchuck, in *How to Manage Conflict in the Church*, has called the three P's of conflict management:

Permission: Everyone involved must be told that disagreements are okay. No one should feel guilty about offering a dissenting view.

Potency: Each person must be allowed to state his or her position with strength and clarity. There's nothing unhealthy about airing strong feelings as long as we respect one another.

Protection: While it's okay to disagree with one another, no one will be intentionally hurt, nor will anyone be allowed to inflict needless hurt.

Unless these ground rules are openly stated, conflicts will often be prolonged as people avoid the real issues until they feel secure enough to speak up without risking irreparable damage to the church or themselves.

Second, if possible, *reframe the dragons.* The natural response when under attack is to put up defenses, if not visibly, at least emotionally. We're hurt, and like any injury, our hurt makes us more sensitive to the slightest pressure. Things that before wouldn't have bothered us now make us recoil.

Reframing how we see the dragons can help keep us from overreacting.

One Sunday when Rob Carlson stepped into the pulpit, his glance fell upon the Millers in the fifth row—Mike on one end, Erika on the other, and four kids in between. Suddenly Rob found his mouth dry, he couldn't seem to breathe, and he couldn't remember what he'd intended to say.

The Millers were irregular attenders, but they had started a Bible study in their home and were teaching some things in direct conflict with the church's statement of faith. Rob had had some bad experiences with outside groups preying on church people in the past, and he feared the Millers would make their way through the congregation spreading unrest if not outright heresy.

Something had to be done. He didn't know what he was going to say, but he had made an appointment to visit the

Miller home Tuesday evening. He wasn't looking forward to the encounter.

He managed to get through his sermon, but his delivery was rough, disjointed. He doubted if many people sensed his discomfort, but he knew he wasn't getting through.

Afterward Jeff Duncan, the youth pastor, came into the office and asked, "Was something bothering you today?"

"I was hoping it didn't show," Rob said. He told Jeff about his dread of confronting the Millers. "I looked at them in the pew, and all I saw was two lions on either side of the path. I felt like they were going to devour me, and if not me, then everything else in the church."

"Don't look at them as lions," Jeff said. "Look at them as wounded sheep."

This simple change made a big difference. In a moment, Rob's fear was gone. "I've never taken them out of that frame," he says now, three years later. "Jeff's observation was true, not that the Millers' lives were in disarray, but they had come through some difficult times and needed to be encouraged. I stopped assuming they were prowling lions and assumed they were wounded sheep. I loved them, and when we talked about the Bible study, they happily agreed not to teach those doctrines if those were not in alignment with our church."

The Millers have joined the church, and Rob enjoys a growing relationship with them.

Reframing doesn't change the dragons, but it can change the way we treat them. And sometimes that's enough.

Third, *pray not only about, but for the dragons.* With some difficult people, it's easier to publicize foibles and faults than to pray for them. But when you genuinely pray *for* the person hurting you, a whole new dimension enters.

Samuel offers a marvelous model. He had been the God-appointed judge and unquestioned leader of Israel, but when he was old, the people turned against him, demanding a king instead. Samuel tried to dissuade them. But when they insisted, he didn't resign or shake his fist or whine over his blemished career.

Instead he said, "For the sake of his great name the Lord will not reject his people, because the Lord was pleased to make you his own. As for me, far be it from me that I should sin against the Lord by failing to pray for you. And I will teach you the way that is good and right" (1 Samuel 12:22–23).

Even after his defeat in the "business meeting," Samuel recognized that God's people deserve prayer simply because they are God's. How difficult it must have been to continue to pray and teach. But if he could do it for a nationful of obstinate dragons, might it be possible on behalf of a churchful?

Finally, *be gentle but firm.* If you're a church leader, the authority is on your side and people expect you to take the initiative.

This is particularly necessary with people who want to be the convicting voice of the Holy Spirit for other people's lives. One pastor was taken aside by a young man and told, "You're working in the wrong area. Your spiritual gift is evangelism, not church planting or leadership. You should be on the road as an evangelist."

After two or three of these jabs, the pastor was torn. *Is he right? Am I really doing what God wants me to do?* Because the young man was a sincere and committed worker, the pastor's emotional upheaval was even greater. After two months of self-doubt, the pastor finally said, "I've listened to your advice, and I appreciate your input, but I cannot accept it. It has caused confusion in my life that didn't exist before you spoke, and I don't think God wants us to continue in confusion. If God wanted me to change ministries, he'd probably tell me, wouldn't you think? Especially after you sensitized me to the issue."

The young man accepted the pastor's judgment. He apologized for putting the pastor through two months of turmoil. This rather harmless dragon was tamed largely because of the respectful but firm way he was approached by the pastor.

A tougher situation is when certain church members are devoted to a national religious figure who has different views than the pastor. They want the church's teaching, vocabulary, and style to parallel that of the prominent personality. How can a pastor who speaks to hundreds dare disagree with someone who speaks to hundreds of thousands?

What is the best way to respond? "Attacking the views of the personality does *not* work," says a Nebraska pastor. "The moment you do that, you become the bad guy. You don't have the credibility to attack a 'hero of the faith.' Besides, I appreciate 95 percent of what the celebrity says; it's just the 5 percent and the way people want to apply it in our church that become divisive."

Again, a gentle but firm attitude is the best response. The direction and style of ministry are the responsibility of the pastor and board. In this situation, the battle to be fought is not over the particulars but over the authority and decision-making process in the church.

"The only thing that's worked for us is pointing out that as pastor I, along with our board, have been given the responsibility for this congregation," says the Nebraska pastor. "When we hear them out but gently explain that we have to make hard decisions about what *our* church can do in *our* situation, they accept that more readily."

The spirit needed for confronting dragons is neither one of fear and withdrawal nor one of arrogant power. It is gentleness and firmness—an attitude of smart love.

The Atmosphere for Confronting

The climate of any encounter with dragons can be an important factor in improving or damaging the relationship. A setting where no one is likely to lose face—a private, unhurried conversation—is most effective in restoring relationships. Two important aspects of creating the right atmosphere are timing and location.

The *timing* must be planned with an eye on the emotional barometer. Confrontations are usually precipitated by a particular experience that cannot be ignored, something that makes us say, "Now he's gone too far."

If we respond too quickly, while the emotional barometer still reads too high, both we and the dragon risk not being able to see all sides of the issue clearly enough. The prophet Nathan waited a year after David's sin with Bathsheba before confronting the king. While it probably wasn't a case of Nathan needing to calm down, perhaps it took that long for David to be open to receive Nathan's accusation.

On the other hand, if we wait too long, the unresolved situation can raise the frustration level until we lose emotional control, as Charles Westerman did in chapter 6.

"Before I confront anyone, I call a fellow pastor and talk through the situation," says an experienced minister. "That calms me down, helps me clarify the approach to take, and helps me get my motives straightened out."

The *location* of a meeting can also help or hinder the cause.

Holding a meeting in the pastor's office gives a definite advantage if we want to exert our authority, negotiate from strength, or exercise discipline. It is *our* turf—our desk, our chair, our pictures, our calendar. We can control the seating, and unless there's a separate seating area, we'll probably be in the ultimate power position—behind a desk. Most people who enter will feel they have entered our realm and grant us the right to set the agenda and take the initiative.

It's a good situation for a showdown but probably not the place to build or restore a relationship. It makes many people feel defensive, insecure, unable to open up fully. A Lutheran pastor admitted the breakdown in a relationship with one man in the congregation was partially caused by an office conversation. The man had been overstating his position in church business meetings, and the pastor thought a gentle word about diplomacy would help. But the man misinterpreted the gesture and told his friends the pastor had "tried to silence me."

"I found out later this man had often been called in and reprimanded by his boss at work," says the pastor. "That's how he interpreted my action. Another setting would have helped."

A second option is neutral turf—a restaurant, for instance. While not offering the home field advantage, it proves a better setting for building relationships or negotiating as equals. "I use several coffee shops that have a back table or quiet room where we can have a private conversation," says a Covenant Church pastor. "I always tell them I'm picking up the tab, and we make small talk until we place our orders. Then I bring up the issue we need to discuss. The neutral turf has almost always proven beneficial in working through differences."

A third option is meeting on the other person's home turf. Some pastors report this works best for first getting acquainted with newcomers or, with dragons, when coming to them on their terms. This can be effective when we sense something is wrong and just need to hear them out. Or if we want to take the first step toward reconciliation, or when we need to apologize. In their own house or apartment, people are more likely to feel free to talk, to air their strong emotions. They feel more in control.

Many meetings, of course, are also held at the church—in conference rooms around a table or in the sanctuary pews. These are usually attended by more than two or three people. Each location establishes its own atmosphere.

One principle, however, does seem to hold true whatever the room arrangement: If you anticipate problems from someone at the meeting, sit right next to him or her, rather than across. It is very difficult to argue with someone when you're not in the traditional positions of confrontation. Breaking down the physical distance seems to chip away at the emotional distance.

If you want a direct confrontation, however, sitting directly across from the person is the most effective arrangement.

These are all generalizations, of course, but when dealing with dragons, nonverbal communication plays a larger role than you usually realize.

The Approach to Confronting

The procedure offered by Jesus in Matthew 18 for dealing with "your brother or sister [who] sins"—talking privately, meeting with witnesses, and finally telling it to the church—is also a good order to follow with dragons. But between the private conversation and church action, there are several other intermediate steps that you can take.

Private conversation. Initially, this is not a confrontation but an attempt to understand the other person and see him or her as Christ does. The goal is to emphasize the many ways you are alike, to see some glory in each other's lives. More people are changed by attention and understanding than correction and coercion.

The book *The One-Minute Manager* makes the point well: If you're going to correct someone effectively, every criticism has to be accompanied by a compliment—in the same context and with virtually the same breath. People are more willing to change when they know they're appreciated, understood, and valued.

Then represent your view clearly and concisely. Try to remember your larger mission—to build the whole church body, including this person—and explain the spiritual issues involved.

If the areas of disagreement are significant, a *willingness to bend* is the next step. Some members of a Southern Baptist church in Louisiana were angry with the pastor because the church didn't have a Women's Missionary Union. His past experiences with them had been negative, and he didn't want to drain the energy from the outreach to the unchurched he was emphasizing. When he met with the malcontents, he went willing to bend, willing to adjust to any needs he hadn't seen before. He asked why they felt a WMU was important. "We need Bible study and fellowship for women" was the reply.

"Fine," he said. "Why don't we start a Bible study for women, with child care provided by the church? It will give women a chance to invite their neighbors to take a break from the kids. It will offer fellowship, Bible study, *and* evangelism opportunities."

Everyone was happy with the solution.

The most common mistake in dealing with dragons is approaching them judgmentally, assuming theirs is a sin problem. "I used to say, 'If you don't quit what you're doing, we're going to have to take action against you,'" says an Oregon pastor. "But our first approach should be one of compassion, because nine out of ten sinners in the church are hurting more than we imagine. Now I'll put my arm around a man and say in private, 'Jim, I've heard some things, like . . . Is there any truth to this?' Often he'll break down and acknowledge it. But my key question is 'How can I help you?' It usually takes them by surprise."

If understanding, willingness to bend, and compassion don't work, try at least to *agree on how you'll disagree.*

One outspoken matron, a charter member of an independent congregation in Wisconsin, habitually and openly criticized the pastor's sermons, board decisions, and anything else she didn't care for. She was an accomplished parliamentarian and often used the church constitution to frustrate the desires of the majority.

One day the pastor told her, "Marion, let's agree on one point anyway: When you have a complaint, come to me first. Do not talk to anyone else. Maybe we'll be able to solve the problem without getting the whole church upset." She made the promise.

But within a month, as the pastor suspected she would, she was carping after church about the way the new lines were painted on the parking lot. The pastor invited her into the office. "We've had disagreements in the past, Marion. But one thing I've never accused you of is lying."

"What do you mean?" she asked.

"You promised me you'd see me first with your complaints, and yet you were telling Marlene Hansen your objections to the work in the parking lot."

Marion, an honest person, admitted she broke her promise. Being caught in the act surprised her. She stopped complaining, and within months she was one of the pastor's strongest backers, occasionally to his embarrassment when she continued to use technical parliamentary procedure for his benefit.

Witnesses. Sometimes private conversations, even with all the peacemaking techniques we can muster, are not enough. At that point, witnesses are necessary. Especially if the conflict involves us personally, other people can be used to resolve the problem. Those in the church who are respected by the dissidents and yet willing to defend another position can be effective in confrontations with rampaging dragons.

Pastor Roger Smalley had a policy that he would not perform the wedding ceremony of a Christian marrying a non-Christian. When Roger explained the policy to Ed Hogan's daughter, who wanted to marry a man who had not accepted Christ, Ed was irate. In the adult Sunday school class, he stood up and asked how the pastor could get away with not doing his job and refusing to perform a wedding for a member of the church.

Roger, who wasn't in the class at the time, felt that since he was the object of Ed's wrath, perhaps the Zanders, long-time members of the church and friends of the Hogans, could be more effective peacemakers. Roger explained the reasons behind his policy to the Zanders and asked them to visit Ed.

They did, explaining the biblical instructions against being "unequally yoked" and pointing out that the pastor had counseled many people coming from this kind of spiritual mismatch whose marriages later fell apart. They said the pastor was convinced it was a mistake even from a practical point of view. If the couple was going to get married, they could do so without pretending that it was "a Christian wedding." The Zanders succeeded in getting Ed to concede the pastor did have a point. In time, Ed and the pastor were able to repair their relationship.

At the point private conversations do not resolve the situation and witnesses become involved, two precautions should probably be taken: *begin taking notes* and *inform the board*.

Note taking is a defensive move. Often dragons are in the business of collecting injustices real and perceived. They may charge us with breaking promises, or perhaps they'll later misrepresent conversations.

After the relationship has broken down, pastors should have a witness present in any subsequent extended conversation. But in addition, it is wise to keep a written record of the content of the conversation and any conclusions reached. The lightest ink is better than the strongest memory. Not only does it help both sides keep the facts straight, but it also saves lost sleep trying to recall the order of events if things heat up later on.

As soon as a dispute isn't resolved with personal persuasion, and definitely if any specific action is going to be attempted, it's time to inform the board. Without the support of the board, any action on behalf of the church is impotent if not impossible.

In one Texas church, an elder was very nonchalant about his duties. He stopped attending worship services, and even his attendance at board meetings was sporadic. The rest of the board recognized the problem, but no one was willing to risk losing the man's friendship by confronting him.

The pastor saw no choice but to take action himself. He visited the man and asked about his irregular attendance at church and at board meetings. The elder responded vaguely that he was really busy at work. The pastor suggested that if that was the case and he couldn't fulfill his role as an elder, perhaps he could resign his board position or take another position in the church that didn't require so much time. The encounter seemed to go smoothly, with the elder agreeing to "think it over."

The following day, however, the pastor got several phone calls from church members wanting to know "why you asked Brother Rod to leave the church." The elder and his family left the church "because of the preacher." The next month was spent trying to correct the false rumors.

"My mistake was acting alone," says the pastor. "The situation could have been avoided if I'd insisted that at least one other elder accompany me. If no one was willing, I should have waited until someone was willing. The leadership as a whole must be willing to administer discipline for it to be effective."

Tell it to the church. What do you tell? You do *not* treat the situation as a trial, with the congregation as jury. "Our elders made a mistake by, in essence, *trying* a woman before the congregation," says one Church of Christ minister. "They told specific times, dates, places—and seemed to be building a case, trying to convince the congregation this woman needed discipline. That's the wrong spirit."

What should they have done?

"Explain simply that reconciliation and restoration were needed, and efforts up to this point had not been successful."

Telling the church is not punishment; it is enlisting the help of the whole body in reconciliation. According to the Church of Christ minister, "The spirit needs to be, 'We have dealt personally with this matter and have failed to reconcile. We have gone with two or three others, and that has failed. Now we're taking the next step and asking you, the congregation, to work with us toward restoration. Perhaps you can succeed where we have failed.'"

Treat the person as you would a pagan or tax collector. If the entire church cannot bring reconciliation, the final step, according to Matthew 18, is recognizing that the person is no longer part of the body. Almost always, this is merely an acknowledgment of what has, in fact, already taken place.

"In sixteen years of practicing church discipline," says one West Coast pastor, "we have never reached this step without the person leaving the church on his own, but we still recognize publicly what has happened—that this person is no longer part of us. Not to do so would be tacit acceptance of that person's behavior, and that's hypocrisy—teaching one thing, accepting another."

Treating a person "as a pagan or tax collector," however, is not shaming or despising him. Jesus was known for loving publicans and sinners. But neither did he pretend they were soul mates. This is the delicate balance the church must walk with unrepentant dragons—to love them as outsiders to be won over, but not entrust them with responsibility or pretend that they are members of the body.

In dealing with dragons, public action is a last recourse, obviously. "Never get in a spittin' match with a skunk," says common folk wisdom. "Even if you win, you come out smelling bad." Dragon-pastor conflicts are often like that. Sometimes they can be settled behind the scenes. Or at least they can be settled without a public show of force.

The only time public action is ever appropriate is for continuing, confirmed, and unrelinquished sin—and never unless the leadership of the church supports the move. Bringing things into the open too quickly is more dangerous than waiting too long.

Rather than forcing the issue publicly, often more is gained by learning to minister in an unresolved situation.

11

When There's No Resolution

It is a fact of Christian experience that life is a series of troughs and peaks. In his efforts to get permanent possession of a soul, God relies on the troughs more than the peaks. And some of his special favorites have gone through longer and deeper troughs than anyone else.

Peter Marshall

Are dragons, like the poor, always to be with us? Veteran minister Alan Redpath was once quoted as saying, "If you're a Christian pastor, you're always in a crisis—either in the middle of one, coming out of one, or going into one."

Perhaps contentiousness and factions in the church are inevitable consequences of original sin. But inevitable or not, they disgusted the apostle Paul, who wrote with bitter sarcasm, "No doubt there have to be differences among you to show which of you have God's approval" (1 Corinthians 11:19). A few verses later, his sarcasm set aside, he expresses his feelings directly: "Shall I praise you? Certainly not in this matter!"

Despite our best efforts, the problems of contentious people are not quickly solved. Tensions can linger in limbo, no resolution in sight. Passive resistance, persistent second-guessing, and consumeristic complaint ("this isn't meeting my needs" or "I don't like it") seem to be the twenty-first-century Western world's equivalent to persecution—a continuing threat to the health and growth of the church.

Pastors dealing with dragons must learn to deal with unresolved situations—some temporarily until the dragon is tamed, appeased, or driven off, some indefinitely until we're called to another church, or perhaps until retirement or death.

Pastors have developed a variety of coping strategies to deal with extended periods of frustration.

One writes letters to himself, describing his joys and especially his anxieties. Then he seals them in an envelope and files them unopened, symbolizing his mentally putting them aside.

Another has a continuing email correspondence with three old seminary classmates. They keep one another current on church happenings, write about seemingly unsolvable situations, and describe the latest dragons. "Most of the time," he says, "we're helping each other answer the question 'Am I crazy, or is everyone else?'"

Many seek out another pastor as a prayer partner to evaluate predicaments and encourage each other to persevere.

Besides these and other specific coping techniques, survivors of the dragon wars offer three broader suggestions to those facing the mental anguish of unrelenting opposition.

Give It Time

Time can bring healing. For new pastors, it also often brings an increasing ability to handle dragons.

When Doug and Joan van Arndt accepted the pastorate of a small-town church in Ohio, they didn't expect it to be a cross-cultural experience, but it was. Doug had grown up in a small-town parsonage and felt comfortable with people in small towns, or so he thought. But he hadn't realized that four years of college and three years of seminary, all in metropolitan areas, had changed his tastes in music, reading material, and conversation.

Relationships were the toughest adjustment. The people didn't seem to want a close friendship with the pastor or his family.

"I'd forgotten how people assume a pastor's family is different," he says. "They saw the pastor as a hired hand to maintain the church and perform the services. We felt frozen out of normal friendships."

Their only friends were from the town league basketball team Doug joined and a couple of young mothers Joan met at PTA. None of them were Christians.

Most of the people in the church had been there for years. They knew one another's grandparents and grandchildren. The van Arndts were the youngest family in the congregation, and thus, not only were there educational and cultural gaps but an age gap, too.

Inevitably clashes came over Doug's leadership. His ideas for creative worship elements were dismissed, his proposal for a cooperative Easter sunrise service with other churches in town was quashed, and his sermons were criticized—not enough evangelistic invitations, the board said.

"Why?" asked Doug. "I've spoken personally with everyone in the congregation, and they've all accepted Christ."

"But it warms my heart to hear salvation messages," said the board chairman.

When one older woman criticized Doug publicly in a business meeting for planning a camping trip with the five church youth, Doug asked the church board to speak with her privately in his defense. They refused.

"Joyce was here before you came, and she'll be here after you're gone," one board member replied.

"This is a moving ship," said another. "As long as you do your job and stay away from the steering wheel, you won't have any problems with Joyce or anyone else."

After a year the church voted, for financial reasons, not to raise the pastor's salary. Before the vote, with both Doug and Joan sitting in the meeting, one man stood to say, "We don't need to up the salary. If this isn't enough for the current pastor, we can always get another one to come for even less."

Several months later, Joan broke her leg on the basement stairs. While she was in the hospital, three people came to visit—none from the church. The church ladies sent flowers and a card, but no one came in person.

Doug and Joan were so discouraged they began looking for another church. Doug mailed his resume to three different placement services and his denomination, but no calls came. He contacted one church directly, a congregation of 125 with a pastoral vacancy, and discovered eighteen candidates had applied ahead of him.

Out of a lack of other options, Doug and Joan stayed at the church and endured their frustration. Now, four years later, they're glad they did.

Only now are they finally beginning to feel accepted, though Doug still says he has to get his sense of appreciation and accomplishment from outside interests—basketball, an art class at a nearby college, and community theater. He's starting to see some cohesiveness develop and spiritual growth take place in the Sunday night home Bible study he and Joan lead.

Joan is still not close to any of the ladies, and when she visits college friends and experiences the warmth of those friendships, it's hard to come back to the cool atmosphere at the church. But she, too, is seeing a significant ministry begin with some young families in town. None of them attend their church . . . yet. But Joan senses they're open to the gospel, and she enjoys sharing her life with them.

What can pastors do when they find themselves frozen out? Or in other situations where dragons gain control, how can you break the impasse?

Sometimes time is the only solution—time for new members who aren't bound by the past to help change the spirit of the church, time for certain board members' terms to expire, time for people to understand where the pastor is going and develop enough trust to follow. Pastors report four to eight years are often necessary before people begin to accept them.

"I remember clearly when one gentleman was giving me fits early in my ministry," says a pastor in Tennessee. "One woman said about him, 'I don't think he's right, but he's been a friend for so long.' Well, I had to stay around long enough to be her friend, too. She has since learned to trust me, and she's voted against the gentleman and for me, but it took me eight years to earn that loyalty."

What do we do while waiting for a thaw? Blindly support the status quo? No, we have to stay consistent with our vision for the church even if we lose the decisions. But it helps to learn to lose graciously. "You continue to minister lovingly the way people expect," says one pastor, "but they need to understand it's not the way you want."

Though they are not pawns of the dragons, new pastors recognize that a majority of the people sometimes go along with the dominant personalities because they're familiar, and if the church is going along okay, people would rather not rock the boat. When the new pastor becomes as familiar, his stature rising to the level of the dominant personalities, he will normally develop enough of a following to make a difference.

In the meantime, the task is to minister to the needs people perceive. The perceived needs may not be the genuine ones, of course, but they are needs. By ministering to individuals, by preaching God's Word, by loving the congregation even while losing some battles, we build credibility and contribute to the longevity of the church. And merely maintaining the church is not all bad, even if it isn't everything we want it to be. There's much value in preserving a church body.

Eventually, God willing, we will be able to make the strategic moves to strengthen the body.

Keep Perspective

In addition to patience, a larger perspective helps. Is the opposition really overwhelming? Or is it a vocal minority? Sometimes enlarging the frame of reference helps remind us that one mouth isn't the whole church, one critic isn't the end of our ministry, and even one church isn't the whole body of Christ.

The familiar story of Elijah's hiding from the wrath of Jezebel illustrates the difference between perception and reality. When he despaired that "I, even I only, am left; and they seek my life, to take it away" (1 Kings 19:10 KJV), God pointed out that there were still at least seven thousand non-dragons in Israel.

On an even higher level, it also helps to remind ourselves of God's sovereignty. Anyone who looks closely knows the church's biggest problem is people—sullen, sassy, sometimes savage, always sinful people. But fortunately, while people are the problem, they are not the solution. God is.

If we lose some battles with dragons, what does it matter? It matters to us now, of course, but ultimately it doesn't. Martin Luther, who knew something of church warfare, found comfort in Psalm 118:5–6: "In my anguish I cried to the Lord, and he answered by setting me free. The Lord is with me; I will not be afraid. What can man do to me?" (NIV 1984).

Even when dragons grab a congregation, God is still in control, and he isn't wringing his hands. At times the dragons may win—the ministry of a church may come to a standstill for a generation or more, an individual congregation may disintegrate—but dragons cannot destroy the church. Individual congregations are breakable; the church is not.

Painful though it may be, we must remember that neither our ministry, nor even our church or denomination, is indispensable in God's outworking of history. The *church* is indispensable, but Baptist or Roman Catholic or Presbyterian or Methodist or Nazarene or Episcopal churches are not. At one time, each of them did not exist, and it's conceivable that they may vanish in the future. But God's eternal decrees will remain.

Our job is to remain faithful to the two greatest commandments: to love God with all our heart, soul, mind, and strength, and to love even dragons as ourselves.

Learn Firm Forgiveness

Forgiveness seems like an unlikely tool to use before wars are completely resolved, but the effects of dragons can linger for years, sapping a church's strength, unless the leaders demonstrate strong, visible forgiveness. Even in the midst of unresolved tensions, forgiveness must always be offered.

Patrick Gregg didn't suspect anything was wrong at first. All he knew was that when he and the church chairman authorized payments to the contractor who was building the new educational wing for Garrison Avenue Methodist, church treasurer Dave Akerman seemed reluctant to write the checks. Two weeks after one major payment was due, the check still hadn't been written.

When the contractor called to complain, Patrick phoned Dave, a stockbroker, at his office to ask what had happened to the check.

"I know we're a little overdue, Pastor," Dave said. "I'll get it out. I'm running a bit behind."

"We've got an obligation to pay bills on time," said Patrick. "It's part of our Christian testimony."

"Okay, Pastor."

The next thing Patrick knew, the phone rang again and the board chairman was on the line. He said Dave had just called asking him to get the pastor off his back about the payments.

"He says the money is tied up in CDs," the chairman explained. "If we withdraw it now, it'll cost us an interest penalty. Any way we can hold off for two more weeks until the CDs mature?"

Patrick pointed out that the payment was already two weeks overdue. He wondered silently why Dave hadn't told him about the CDs, but in the end he agreed to ask the contractor for an extension.

The contractor wasn't happy about the delay. He had just paid his workers, and this put him in a cash flow bind, but "I guess we can hold things together for two more weeks. But we definitely need the money then."

Two weeks later, on a Tuesday morning, Patrick got a call from Kevin Hinson, a church member and vice president of the bank where the church kept its accounts.

"Patrick, I think we've got a problem," he said, his voice

serious. "Dave Akerman and I need to talk with you. And you probably better get the board chairman in on this, too."

Patrick couldn't imagine what had happened, but he called the chairman, and two hours later, the four men were seated around the table in Patrick's office. Kevin began.

"Dave told me something today that I insisted he tell you immediately. Dave?"

Dave sat staring at the floor, and when he spoke, his voice shook slightly. "Two months ago, I heard about a great opportunity, a new company that was looking for investors. It was a sure bet. If I worked things right, I figured I could pay off the entire cost of the church's construction. I took the $500,000 in the building fund and invested it in the company's stock. It should have tripled in value within a couple months—we could have had $1.5 million to pay off our construction. It was a terrible mistake. Yesterday I found out the company declared bankruptcy."

Patrick felt his stomach getting queasy. "How much did we lose?"

"We lost it all," said Dave. "We may have a few hundred dollars from recent offerings in the building fund, but the $500,000 is gone. I'm sorry. It was bad judgment on my part."

Bad judgment?! Patrick wanted to scream. *How dare you take the entire building fund without telling anyone and invest it in some shady deal? Do you know what you've done to us? We owe the contractor an overdue $100,000, we've got nothing to pay it with, and the building is barely half done. You've just crippled us.*

Instead, Patrick said nothing, groping for words. The room was silent. None of them had any answers.

Finally he said, "This is too much to digest right now. Let's get the board together tonight, and in the meantime, let's pray for wisdom and resiliency, and maybe a miracle."

After Dave left, Patrick got more details from Kevin. Since building fund checks required two signatures, apparently Dave had been able to transfer funds to another church account that required only one. Kevin had only heard about it that morning when Dave came in asking for a loan, intending to borrow money personally to reinvest and try to recover his losses. Kevin eventually got the story out of him and demanded he tell the pastor right away.

"Even if he had made a killing on the market, how do we know he would have returned the money to the church?" Kevin asked. "He sure was slick in the way he secretly juggled funds to get them under his sole control."

Patrick just shrugged. "We're not judges of the man's motives. Only God can do that." But privately he shared Kevin's suspicions.

That night, Patrick was amazed and pleased at the way the board responded. Yes, they were shocked. Yes, they were outraged. Yes, they were worried. But their focus was "What should Christians do in this situation?" Their immediate concern was the overdue $100,000. All twelve board members agreed to borrow money, take out home equity loans, cash in savings accounts, whatever it took to pay the contractor. They'd worry about the longer-range effects later.

They approached several other families in the church, and people responded, putting second mortgages on their homes, giving money saved for children's education or their own retirement. By Friday, Patrick gave the contractor a check for $100,000.

The second concern was what to do with Dave. The board agreed that he should step down immediately as treasurer. But they did not want to press legal charges against him.

"The church is not in the business of putting people in prison," said one board member. "We're in the redemptive business."

Several people asked, "Is he sorry for what he did, or sorry he was caught?"

One man asked, "Is it true repentance if he doesn't make restitution?" Dave had never even offered to try to repay the debt. But others responded, "Realistically, could he ever raise $500,000? Probably not." The point was discussed at length.

In the end, however, the board identified three options: (1) skinning Dave alive and pressing legal charges, (2) officially forgiving but continuing to hold it against him personally, or (3) forgiving and taking steps to develop a normal relationship.

The board agreed that the church's responsibility was to forgive, even though Dave's repentance left something to be desired. They also authorized Patrick to set up an appointment for Dave with a professional counselor to work on his admitted impulse control problem.

That Sunday Patrick preached from Matthew 18:21–35 on the need to forgive if we are to be forgiven. Dave was sitting in the second row. Patrick explained the situation, naming names and amounts, and pointing out that they would easily have forgiven someone taking and losing $100. In this situation, the amount was greater but the principle the same.

He also said, "If someone had done this at another church, been thrown out, and came to this church, we wouldn't refuse to minister to that person. No, we'd say, 'Here's a person who needs our love.' We don't agree with what he's done, but he needs the ministry of Christ, the ministry of restoration. If that is true, why can't the church where the sin occurs provide it? We don't want sinners feeling they have to leave and go to a different church. We are a family, and we'll take care of our own."

After the benediction, Patrick felt a visible symbol of the forgiveness was needed, so he walked down to the second row and hugged Dave to signal the rest of the congregation that he was not to be ostracized.

In the weeks that followed, there was some grumbling among the congregation that Dave hadn't done enough to make up for his act. The church, which had always been financially healthy, was now operating at a deficit, and since so many had given large gifts to make the building payment, the weekly offerings often did not cover operating expenses.

One man asked Patrick, "Can you honestly say you don't still have the urge to punch Dave in the nose?" Patrick admitted he still felt anger.

"Isn't that hypocrisy, then, to say you forgive him?"

"No, I don't think so," said Patrick thoughtfully. "Is it hypocrisy when you feel like having an affair but resist the temptation because you know it's not right? Yes, I'm tempted to refuse to forgive, but I know that Christians need to behave another way. Hypocrisy or integrity is determined by what you decide, not what you want."

Now, three years later, the church continues to struggle financially. The building project has been completed and paid for, but at great cost to the giving power of the congregation. The church has, however, learned what firm forgiveness is and what it requires.

All the dragons mentioned in this book can do significant harm—financially, emotionally, spiritually. They can foul the atmosphere and vitality of the church. But they must be forgiven. Not to forgive violates Christ's command in Matthew 6:14–15 and puts our own ability to be forgiven in doubt.

But what is forgiveness, especially forgiving dragons? We must be clear what it is not.

Forgiveness is not giving in and agreeing with them. If we're right (and hopefully we are), then the dragons are probably wrong! Forgiveness needn't sacrifice truth.

Nor is forgiveness giving them our complete trust—they may not be trustworthy. Putting Dave in charge of another $500,000 of church funds would not have been forgiveness but foolishness.

Nor is forgiveness forgetting. Forgetting is more a result of a short memory or subconscious suppression, while forgiving is an act of the will, a difficult and disciplined decision to love the sinner while hating the sin. In fact, remembering dragons' tendencies in the past, we are better able to love them and prevent the same mistakes in the future.

What then is forgiveness?

Forgiveness at bottom is a new beginning, starting at the present moment, the present situation. You don't start where you wish you were but at the place where you are. Together you begin again.

The Greek word used in the Bible for forgiveness, *aphiemi*, literally means "to let go"—to let go of resentment, of anger, of all those feelings of revenge that are so tempting to hold close. Forgiveness is not leaving a dragon with something to live down but offering to live through the situation together.

True forgiveness, even when forgiving a dragon, is saying, "I don't completely understand you. I can't excuse what's happened, and I can't forget what you've done. But here's my hand. I want to be your friend again. I still want to work with you. Let's begin over."

That offer must always be on the table, and frequently spoken, even while the dragon is refusing to reconcile. God is in the business of new beginnings. To be about our Father's business means we must be, too.

Epilogue

It was good for me to be afflicted so that I might learn your decrees.

Psalm 119:71

Pachomius is hardly a household name. His face has never graced the cover of a magazine. But for Christians afflicted with difficult people, the life of this obscure Egyptian soldier offers unexpected encouragement.

Conscripted into the military, Pachomius was won to Christ by the kindness of Christians in Thebes. After his release from the military around AD 315, he was baptized. Serious about his new faith and determined to grow, Pachomius became a disciple of Palamon, an ascetic who taught him the self-denial and solitary life of a religious hermit.

In early Christianity, the model of devotion was the recluse, dedicated to resisting the corruption of society. Trying to avoid the contagion of sins material and sensual, these men (such severe sanctification was almost exclusively male) would wander the desert alone—fasting, praying, and having visions. Many went to extremes: eating nothing but grass, living in trees, or refusing to wash. Often their reputations attracted large crowds.

The most famous, some years later, was Simeon Stylites, the austere anchorite who was so distracted by people trespassing his cave that he built and lived atop a pillar for thirty-six years, fed by disciples who lifted baskets of food sixty feet to their lofty leader. Ironically, thousands came to hear the preaching of this elevated man of God.

Such was the popular image of holiness: solitude, silence, and severity. And such was Pachomius's early spiritual training. But he began to question the methods and lifestyle of his mentors. He wondered:

How can you learn humility living alone?

How can you learn kindness or gentleness or goodness in isolation?

How can you learn patience unless someone puts yours to the test?

How can you learn to love if no one else is around?

In short, he concluded, developing Christian virtues demands other people—ordinary, ornery people. "To save souls," he said, "you must bring them together."

True love isn't even learned among friends we have chosen. God's kind of love is best learned where we can't be selective about our associates. Perhaps this is why the two institutions established by God—the family and the church—are not joined by invitation only. We have no choice about who our parents or brothers or sisters will be, yet we are expected to love them. Neither can we choose who will or will not be in the family of God; any who confess Jesus as their Lord must be welcomed. We learn *agape* love most effectively in our involuntary associations, away from the temptation of choosing to love only the attractive.

So Pachomius began an ascetic *koinonia,* where holiness was developed not in isolation but in community. Instead of each person seeking God in his own way, with the dangers of idleness and eccentricity, Pachomius established a common life based on worship, work, and discipline. This was the beginning of genuine monastic life.

In community with flawed, sometimes disagreeable people, followers of Pachomius learned to take hurt rather than give it. They discovered that disagreements and opposition provide the opportunity to redeem life situations and experience God's grace.

Or, as Thomas à Kempis would say years later in *The Imitation of Christ*, "It is good that we at times endure opposition and that we are evilly and untruly judged when our actions and intentions are good. Often such experiences promote humility and protect us from vainglory. For then we seek God's witness in the heart."

Pachomius has been largely forgotten in church history, but for modern-day believers beset by dragons, he can be adopted as a patron saint. He pointed out that as attractive as solitary sanctification may seem, it is life among the dragons that develops the qualities God requires.

Notes

Chapter 4: Electronic Warfare

1. Daniel Kurtzman, "Michael Brown's Idiotic Emails," About.com, November 3, 2005, http://politicalhumor.about.com/b/2005/11/03/michael-browns-idiotic-emails.htm.

2. Raymond A. Friedman and Steven C. Currall, "Conflict Escalation: Dispute Exacerbating Elements of E-Mail Communication," *Human Relations* Volume 56(11) (2003): 1325–1347, www.owen.vanderbilt.edu/vanderbilt/data/research/337full.pdf.

3. Jody Bruner, "Email Disputes: How to Avoid Conflict Escalation," *Brunerbiz,* July 3, 2009, www.brunerbiz.com/2009/07/email-disputes-how-to-avoid-conflict-escalation/.

Chapter 5: When the Mind Isn't Quite Right

1. "Statistics," National Institute of Mental Health, www.nimh.nih.gov/statistics/1anydis_adult.shtml.

2. Amy Simpson, *Troubled Minds: Mental Illness and the Church's Mission* (Downers Grove, IL: InterVarsity, 2013), 37.

3. Ibid., 33–35.

4. "What Is Mental Illness?" National Alliance on Mental Illness, www.nami.org/Template.cfm?Section=By_Illness.

5. Amy Simpson, *Troubled Minds*, 53.

6. Ibid., 54.

7. Ibid., 101.

8. Ibid., 37.

9. Dietrich Bonhoeffer, *Life Together* (New York: HarperCollins, 1954), 86.

10. Henri Nouwen, *The Living Reminder: Service and Prayer in Memory of Jesus Christ* (New York: HarperCollins, 1977), 48–49.

Chapter 7: The Best Defense

1. Marshall Shelley and Dean Merrill, "The Pastor's Passages," *Leadership Journal*, Fall 1983.

Marshall Shelley is a vice president of Christianity Today International and the author of several books, including *Helping Those Who Don't Want Help* and *The Leadership Secrets of Billy Graham*. He holds a journalism degree from Bethel University in Minnesota and an MDiv from Denver Seminary in Colorado. Marshall and his family live in Illinois.